Hitching a Ride
THE UNSOLVED MURDER OF DANA BRADLEY

Hitching a Ride

THE UNSOLVED MURDER OF DANA BRADLEY

by Darrin McGrath

Flanker Press Ltd.
St. John's, Newfoundland
2003

National Library of Canada Cataloguing in Publication

McGrath, Darrin Michael, 1966-
    Hitching a ride : the unsolved murder of Dana Bradley / by Darrin McGrath.

ISBN 1-894463-44-7

    1. Bradley, Dana, d. 1981. 2. Murder--Newfoundland and Labrador--St. John's. I. Title.

HV6535.C33S3534   364.15'23'097181   C2003-905488-8

Cover design by
Dale Wilson Photography

Printed in Canada by
Friesens

Flanker Press Ltd.
P.O. Box 2522, Station C
St. John's, Newfoundland A1C 6K1
Toll Free: 1-866-739-4420
Telephone: (709) 739-4477
Fax: (709) 739-4420

E-mail: info@flankerpress.com
www.flankerpress.com

For Ann

Preface

Researching the unsolved murder of Dana Nicole Bradley was difficult to write for a variety of reasons. Primarily, the subject matter is distressing: the brutal slaying of a fourteen year-old little girl. Emotionally, this was a tough book to author. The details haunted me, however, it was a story that begged to be told.

Initially, I set out to write a book of several true crime stories, thinking I'd deal with two or three cases. As I delved into the newspaper coverage of the events beginning on December 14, 1981, when Dana first disappeared, I realized that this case was a book unto itself.

As I read about the unsolved murder, many questions arose. Who killed Dana and why? Was the killer still living in the St. John's area? Was the killer still alive? How had the killer been able to escape the combined efforts of the Royal Canadian Mounted Police and the Royal Newfoundland Constabulary? These questions remain unanswered.

Great respect had to be given to the fact that the Dana Nicole Bradley case is an unsolved homicide. It is a major, serious crime. Investigators were limited in what they could say and reveal. Many questions directed to police officials had to be left unanswered simply because they involved aspects of a capital crime that might someday have to be dealt with in a court of law. Much of the book is therefore based on interviews with friends and teachers, plus newspaper and magazine clippings of the crime.

Some people declined interviews about the events of December 1981 and the aftermath. Obviously, this was such a distressing time for them personally. Likewise some eyewitnesses were reluctant to talk.

I was fortunate to interview two people who went to school with Dana and knew her well. In order to afford them a level of protection from the glare of the public spotlight, they appear in this volume simply as a friend of Dana's, or as Dana's friend Terri. It is hoped the reader will understand the reasons for permitting them this level of anonymity. I tried to remain objective, but it was difficult interviewing these two sources about their deceased friend.

I attempted to speak with as many people connected to the case as I could. However, I did not ask to formally interview Dana's mother and stepfather. I did speak with Dana's stepfather on the phone about this project, so that it's release would not come as a surprise, and to give him the opportunity to discuss any issues or concerns. I assured him that the book would just present the facts of the case in a non-sensational manner, and hopefully, I have achieved that goal.

Like the old saying "no man is an island" there are a great many people I need to thank for their help and assistance with this project. First, my wife Ann put up with me throughout the long months I toiled on this book. Her encouragement, patience and editorial work are gratefully appreciated.

My mother, Mary, was a steadfast supporter during the course of this project. My brother Jim was a tower of strength when mine sagged. My sister Marilyn provided much insight based on her knowledge of the case. My other siblings, Rosemarie and Pat also helped and encouraged me. My sister-in-law Janet and my brother-in-law David both aided me in establishing contacts with friends of Dana they knew. My cousin Chris talked with me about Dana and then gave me leads on her close friends. Thanks also to Dave and Mary Lou Stinson.

A great many of my friends bolstered my spirits and talked with me about the book during the coldest, stormiest months of the winter. In no particular order I wish to thank the following friends of mine: Dominic Reardon; Tom Cantwell; John Dillon; Frank Warren; George Power; Steve Chafe; Bob Woolridge; Sean Kelly; Steve Hood; Craig Westcott; From Flanker Press, Garry Cranford for numerous cups of coffee; Jerry Cranford for editing and designing; Margo Cranford, Vera McDonald, and Laura Cameron for editing.

Thanks to Royal Canadian Mounted Police Constable Christine "Chris" MacNaughton. Cst. MacNaughton is currently one of the lead investigators on the Dana Bradley file and she spent much time assisting me with this project.

Thanks to all the interview subjects for this book, especially Fred Tulk, Dana's school principal, and Glenda Cluett, Dana's grade nine teacher. Each of these educators offered tremendous insights about Dana and the effect her murder had on the school.

Thanks to Bill Callahan, former publisher of *The Daily News*; Pat Doyle, retired reporter with *The Evening Telegram*;

Mayor Andy Wells, City of St. John's; Paul Mackey, Director of Public Works, City of St. John's; Neachel Keeping, St. John's City Archives; the staff of the A.C. Hunter Library, Newfoundland Room.

Thanks to Mark Dwyer, Managing Editor, *The Newfoundland Herald*, for arranging access to the *Herald's* archives. A great big thank you to Scott Dwyer of *The Herald*, for technical help with photos.

Thanks also to Vince Hempsall, Managing Editor of *The Downhomer* magazine.

I also wish to acknowledge the assistance of Jim Wellman, Managing Editor, of *The Navigator* magazine.

I am indebted to Harry Smeaton who witnessed Dana being picked up on Topsail Road on December 14, 1981 and who told me about that night.

A special thank you to Jack Lavers, retired RCMP Inspector, who patiently answered my many questions.

Hats off to Richard Rogers, LL.B., of Williams, Roebothan, McKay, Marshall. Richard was a great resource person and provided useful advice and support. Also to Dr. Elliott Leyton, author of *Hunting Humans*.

I am obliged to offer a very special thank you to Dana's friend Terri, and Dana's school friend, who made time to speak with me about the most awful of events. Their courage and honesty was and is greatly appreciated.

Finally, for the help of many other people unnamed, thanks.

If there are errors, they are mine alone.

Darrin McGrath
19 August 2003

The Ghost of Dana Bradley
Is standing sadly on the road to home,
You can see her as you hurry by,
Pale against the evening sky;
She stands alone,
Thumb out to hitch a ride,
Swallowing her young girl's pride like a bitter wine,
Counting on a kind heart.
There's a gamble at the start in these times.

Depending on the kindest heart,
Could be a gamble at the start in these times.

Excerpt from "The Ghost of Dana Bradley" by Ron Hynes
Recorded on the CD Get Back Change: Borealis: 2003

Used with permission, Ron Hynes and Dawn Bradley.

There's an old saying in St. John's that the Southside Hills can predict the weather. When the Hills look close and foreboding, a snowfall can be expected.

It's a pity the Southside Hills can't talk. What a story they could tell.

One

In December of 1981, 14-year-old hitchhiker Dana Nicole Bradley stepped into a car on Topsail Road and was never seen alive again.

THE DAY STARTED OUT as just another routine day in St. John's, capital city of Newfoundland and Labrador. The weather that day was fairly mild with temperatures hovering from -2 to +1, and although the sky was overcast, no rain or snow fell.

St. John's, with a population of 90,000 was a bustling seaport with a sheltered harbour in its downtown section. All types of vessels use the harbour, from commercial fishing vessels to goods-carrying container ships to oil exploration ships. The relatively peaceful nature of Newfoundland society made the events of December 1981 all the more distressing. The rate of violent crimes, particularly homicide, was relatively low and an infrequent phenomenon in Newfoundland, with no clear pattern or trend.

IT WAS ELEVEN DAYS before Christmas, and for most people thoughts were focused on the coming holiday season and what remained to be done for the celebrations on the twenty-fifth. For the students and teachers of I.J. Samson Junior High School, on Bennett Avenue in St. John's, there were just a few days left before Christmas holidays. A school dance was planned for the end of the week, to celebrate the season.

Dana Bradley was a grade nine student at I.J. Samson. She was a pretty girl with blue eyes and a fair complexion, her face framed by shoulder-length, dark blond hair.

Ms. Glenda Cluett was Dana Bradley's homeroom teacher and also taught the intelligent young girl math and French.

"She was a good-looking girl," Glenda recalls. "She was always well dressed – classily dressed – and she kept herself immaculately clean. Dana wore a bit of eyeshadow – she always wore nice things. I think she always wore a locket, heart-shaped. And I remember she had a very nice, delicate bracelet."

Dana and most of the girls in her grade nine class could have passed for seventeen or eighteen. The teenage girls seemed more mature than most of the boys in that grade, and because they were so attractive, Dana and some of her girlfriends drew the attention of boys who were in grade ten or eleven.

A former I.J. Samson student describes Dana as a fun-loving, very outgoing person. "Dana was always friendly. She was helpful and would lend her notes to people who had missed classes. She was popular, but not snobby. She had lots of friends throughout the three levels of the student body."

Dana was at the age where, like many of her classmates, "for the first time, life was turning her head instead of school books."

Despite the usual distractions, Dana was good at the books. Glenda Cluett recalls that she was an excellent student. "Dana was a brainy girl and was good academically. She was doing advanced math, which I taught, and she was very artistic. It was around Christmastime, and Dana was doing a mural on the back wall of the classroom, featuring Charlie Brown and Peanuts. She'd stay after school and work on it, or work on it during lunchtime." While Ms. Cluett does not remember Dana ever telling her that she wanted to enter one of the more typical, traditional professional fields for women, she "... couldn't imagine her not doing something good, career-wise."

When Dana was in grade seven, she attempted to earn her way into the Guinness Book of World Records for holding a smile for the longest time. A schoolmate recalled her tenacity and drive. "She kept smiling all day, until she got an earache, and had to stop." Even though Dana's attempt at the world record for the longest-held smile was unsuccessful, she did get her picture in the local newspaper.

How many grade nine students dream of making their mark in the Guinness Book of World Records? How many of those with such dreams actually try to pull it off? It seems that Dana was a girl with vision and a sense of the world around her, and wanted to establish herself and enjoy life while doing it. She had the self-awareness and work ethic to make her dreams a reality.

Her homeroom teacher recalls that in grade nine the female students tended to be much more mature than the young boys. However, "the girls would be bouncing off the walls before Christmas," Glenda Cluett says. "Then it seemed they settled down a lot more after Christmas."

Dana, like her girlfriends, had a bit of youthful wildness in her. On one occasion, Dana's mother had gone away for a weekend, and she had told her mother she'd stay with a friend, Penny Cobb. However, Penny had told her parents that she'd be staying over with Dana. The two threw a big party at the Bradley house, and when Dana's mother came home, she found out about it and was livid. Ms. Cluett remembers Mrs. Bradley's anger at Dana for throwing this party without permission.

"She (Dana) was at that age of being a bit rebellious. She was wild, in a typical teenage sort of way. She was up to all kinds of devilment, like pipping off school."

On the day Dana went missing, the teacher caught her with a note from her mother. Dana was using it to copy the handwriting style onto another note, to explain her absence on a day she had played truant. Glenda Cluett talked to Dana after school and reprimanded her for this behaviour.

"I called her in, and was I mad at her! I warned her about this note business and pipping off. I upset her and she left the classroom crying. So maybe Dana may not have liked me too much for being on her back about pipping off."

AFTER SCHOOL, Dana, a friend Terri, and Penney Cobb hitchhiked to Terri's house and from there Dana and Penny went to the Cobb house on Currie Place, a cul-de-sac off Topsail Road, west of the Village Mall.

Dana's friend Terri recalls the time. "I was in grade nine with Dana. Myself and Dana had grown up together. We met Penny in junior high school. That day, myself, Dana, and Penny hitchhiked home from school and we went to my house for a while. Then Dana and Penny went to Penny's house. I think it was Dana's mother's birthday and Penny said that Dana asked for some money for the bus when she was leaving."

Penny Cobb was interviewed in 1989 by *Newfoundland Lifestyle* magazine about what she recalled regarding the day Dana disappeared. "I don't very often think of that day. I'd broken up with my boyfriend. Dana came over, and she called him up," Cobb said.

It seems that young Dana was going to try and play matchmaker and get them back together. As young friends do, the two girls probably whiled away the afternoon listening to music and chit-chatting. It is certain that neither girl could have imagined the awful events that would soon take place.

Penny Cobb has since married and has children of her own. She remembers Dana as a pretty, popular girl who smiled a lot. "Dana was typical, just like the rest of us." Hitchhiking was something the girls had just started to do, and at the time, it was common practice for students to stand in front of the bus stops and hitchhike.

Around 5:00 P.M. Dana called her grandmother to say that she was on her way home to 160 Patrick Street. Dana's father, William Bradley, and her mother Dawn had gone their separate ways, but Dana lived with her mother. Dawn Bradley was now seeing Jeff Levitz, whom she later married. A little get-together was planned for that evening to celebrate Dawn's birthday, which was the next day. No doubt Dana wanted to be home on time for dinner. Mother and daughter were best friends and had a great relationship. Dawn Bradley adored her little girl.

Dana left the safety of Penny Cobb's home. "She was going to get the bus, but apparently she didn't have any money. Or so I heard since, but I can't remember us even discussing it. It [hitchhiking] was a wrong thing to do, but we didn't think about it then."

Hitchhiking was a "new thing" with the circle of friends who Dana and Penny hung out with. "Whatever possessed us to start, I don't remember," Cobb stated. "I guess it was like everything else, like starting to smoke. Everybody did it, you know. When you're young you do all sorts of stupid things."

It was normal for students to come out of I.J.Samson School, walk down Bennett Avenue to LeMarchant Road and "put the thumb out." Students took the first ride that came along, whether it was the bus or a car that stopped. After school, many students going to the Village Mall took whatever ride came along.

To teenagers, hitchhiking was a way of being independent, of expressing their developing maturity and young adulthood. To some, it was simply a more practical decision, a way to get around without cost.

The implicit innocence of the girls who hitchhiked is readily understood. This was St. John's, not Toronto or Detroit. The youngsters felt confident and safe, and seldom considered the potential dangers involved in hitching a ride with a stranger.

We'll never know exactly what was in Dana's head as she left Currie Place and began to walk along Topsail Road toward home. Was she thinking about Penny and her boyfriend and if they'd get back together? Did she recall something that Terri reminded her of that afternoon? Was she looking forward to the dance to be held at I.J. Samson later in the week, to start off the school Christmas holiday? She was no doubt thinking of her mother; after all, she had called to say she'd be home soon.

When Dana called her family to let them know she was on the way home, the last thing she said to her grandmother was, "I love you."

On Topsail Road, almost directly across the street from McDonald's, and not far from Penny and Terri's homes, Dana Bradley stuck out her thumb for a ride. She was wearing a blue sweater, jeans and cowboy boots, and over the sweater, a blue ski jacket with navy stripes on the sleeves.

AROUND 5:20 P.M., a rusting four-door car, thought to be either a mid-1970's Dodge Dart or Plymouth Valiant, tan or faded yellow in colour, stopped for the young hitchhiker. Dana was seen approaching the car. She tried the handle on the passenger side, but the door refused to open, as if some unforeseen force was trying to warn off the youngster and prevent her from entering the death trap. The driver leaned across the front seat and opened the door from the inside. It swung open and Dana got in. The rusting car headed east on Topsail Road toward the Village Mall. Dana vanished.

IT'S CHILLING TO THINK that on one of the busiest streets in St. John's, opposite a popular good-time family restaurant, a young girl was picked up, never to be seen alive again.

Even as Dana disappeared, families were inside the restaurant, enjoying their meals, sharing their French fries, chatting and joking among themselves. Next door, caffeine lovers were warming themselves and relaxing at Tim Horton's with a cup of coffee and a cigarette. Others were picking up items in a nearby convenience store.

None of them could have imagined that across the street, in full sight of everyone, a pretty little girl was being abducted and about to be brutally murdered.

In 1981, Topsail Road was one of two main arteries beginning in the west and leading to the downtown centre of St. John's. In the area from which Dana Bradley was picked up, there were numerous small businesses, a large shopping mall, several restaurants and new housing subdivisions. It was a growing, prosperous section of St. John's and was totally different in form and shape than the older parts of the city clustered near the harbourfront.

Two

BY 8:30 P.M. Dawn Bradley was very worried that Dana hadn't shown up for supper. She was sure that something had happened to her only child. After all, she had called from Penny Cobb's house to say she was on her way home.

When Dana failed to arrive, her mother became convinced that something terrible had happened. "It just wasn't like her; she wasn't like that," she said in a 1989 interview. Taking Dana's school picture, she went to the Village Mall, a popular hangout for teenagers. Dawn Bradley's hopes of locating her daughter at the mall were squashed. None of the people she approached could recall seeing Dana that evening. She returned home and waited for her fiancé Jeff Levitz to arrive.

Dawn Bradley spoke to Dana's friend Terri. "Mrs. Bradley called again later – she was getting worried. Dana was a very vibrant, bubbly girl with lots of life. She was so close to her mom, they were like best friends. Dana was an only child and was like the apple of her mom's eye."

One can only try to imagine the upset and torment Dawn Bradley was beginning to experience. Unfortunately, this poor woman's mental anguish was just starting.

When Jeff Levitz arrived on Patrick Street, he and Dawn set off to look for the young woman. They searched Cowan Avenue, Bowring Park, the Southside Road, Kilbride, and The Goulds. They stopped at a couple of convenience stores along the way and showed Dana's picture to the staff inside. At one store the lady behind the counter said, "My God, you must be worried to death." The search for Dana was futile, so they proceeded to the police station, headquarters of the Royal Newfoundland Constabulary (RNC).

In a 1992 interview, Jeff Levitz talked about their efforts. "We actually went to the police that evening, and of course ... the police won't take a missing-persons report for at least twenty-four hours. We said, well, this is not a usual case. Dana is missing. She has not gone to a friend's. She has not run away. There wasn't an argument."

Jeff Levitz initially felt that the police didn't believe them. "I'm sure that was the case," Levitz replied. "I mean people just don't go missing. You know ... I'm sure it was the furthest thing from their mind."

Dawn Bradley related a similar tale of police initially not being too concerned with the first report of the overdue teenager. Dawn was treated fine by the officer to whom she reported the problem, but "as soon as (one officer) found out she was an only child, he just got up and left the room." Mrs. Bradley thought at this point that the policeman saw her as an over-anxious mother and that her daughter was just late because she was out with friends, or for some other innocuous reason.

The police did file a report on Dana, but said that not much could be done that night. Meanwhile, Jeff Levitz tried to stay optimistic that everything would work out.

On Topsail Road and on the Maddox Cove Road, not far away, normally commonplace events were being witnessed, but no heed of their import was realized until later. At this point, these witnesses had no inkling of the horror that was about to unfold. However, maternal instincts told Dawn that her daughter was in real trouble.

THE WEATHER THE FOLLOWING DAY, Tuesday, was cloudy and generally mild, with temperatures ranging from -2 to +1. First thing in the morning, Dawn Bradley travelled the short distance from Patrick Street to her daughter's school in the heart of the west end of St. John's. Brightly coloured houses are nestled along quiet but busy streets. St. Clare's and the Grace hospitals stood nearby, like silent, reassuring sentinels, ever ready to assist the sufferer. Corner stores, pharmacies and mature trees all contributed to the sense of community that surrounded both Patrick Street and the school. There was an inherent smallness and sense of togetherness that made this area, like most of St. John's, seem non-threatening and safe.

I.J. Samson had a close-knit student body, with only three levels: seven, eight and nine. It was upsetting to think that a young student was missing from this friendly, pleasant school setting and safe neighbourhood.

Dawn Bradley's thoughts must have been racing as she climbed the school steps the next morning. Mrs. Annie King ran the school cafeteria, and was a family friend of the Bradleys. Her face must have been a welcome sight for the anguished mother. Unfortunately, Mrs. King could offer her no help. There were no reassuring words such as "Yes, I saw Dana here earlier this morning" or "she just left with a few of her friends."

Having found no sign of Dana or helpful information at school, Dawn Bradley returned to the police station where her concerns were treated more seriously; Dana had now been missing overnight.

Despite the policeman's reassurance that they had never had a murder in any cases of missing or overdue persons, Dawn Bradley was certain that her daughter had met with foul play. "I knew she was dead. Otherwise she would have been home."

Dana's friend Terri also went to the police headquarters. "The next day I went to the police station and was down there quite a bit, going over events of the day. That week I was constantly going to the police station."

At this stage of the missing-persons case, the Royal Newfoundland Constabulary was handling the case, since Dana's disappearance fell within their jurisdiction. The RCMP would have been advised of her status as a missing person, but the primary investigators at this juncture were the Constabulary.

ON WEDNESDAY, Dana Bradley's picture, accompanied by a description of her appearance, was published for the first time in both St. John's daily newspapers.

POLICE CONCERNED FOR GIRL'S SAFETY, read the front-page headline in *The Daily News.*

Dana's picture ran under the banner THIS GIRL IS MISSING AND POLICE ARE CONCERNED in *The Evening Telegram.*

These would not be the last times Dana Bradley's smiling face appeared in the newsprint of Newfoundland's capital city.

Dana was five feet, five inches tall, weighing about 110 pounds and having blue eyes and a fair complexion. Her hair was described variously, as dark blond in colour or dark brown.

The police were asking for anyone who had seen Dana or knew anything about her whereabouts to contact the Royal Newfoundland Constabulary at 722-5111.

Detective Lloyd Ford of the RNC's general investigation section was handling the case. He told the papers, "We get reports of lots of missing people, but this one we're treating a lot more seriously than most." Police knew that the girl had phoned her grandmother to say she was on her way home, indicating this was no ordinary case of a young girl running away from home. Ominously, both papers noted that Dana Bradley was known to hitchhike.

THE DAY DANA'S PICTURE and a plea for assistance on her whereabouts appeared in the local papers, Harry Smeaton was sitting down to supper.

"My cousin was reading the paper, and when he was finished he gave it to me," Harry Smeaton recalls. "I saw her picture; it jumped out at me. I said, 'I think we saw this girl.'"

Harry called his brother John and asked him if he had seen the paper. John replied, "Harry, I've already called the police."

Three

GLENDA CLUETT REMEMBERS that "at first I thought Dana might just have taken off on a lark. She had no fear ... she was brave enough to try anything. I thought she might have even gone across the island, or gone to Toronto."

Others, however, thought that something was wrong right from the start. Since Dana had been at a close friend's house, and had called in advance to say she'd be home soon, it didn't make sense for her to go missing. She had a good relationship with her mom, and calling home was a normal, thoughtful thing for her to do.

"As the week wore on," Cluett says, "I was worried because there was no word from Dana to her family."

Not only was Glenda worried about Dana, she was now wondering if reprimanding Dana on Monday afternoon about "pipping off" and falsifying sick notes had something to do with her being missing. After all, Dana had left the classroom crying.

Glenda's concern for Dana increased with the continued media coverage of the girl's disappearance.

School Principal Fred Tulk was also very concerned that Dana was so long overdue and that she had reportedly been hitchhiking. "When she first disappeared, I might have thought that at that age kids sometimes take off. You might get one or two students a year who run away. But if they ran away, usually they were found quickly."

Tulk volunteered in the search. With two Constabulary officers, he went to the Village Mall, asking young people the educator knew from school if they had seen Dana. The trio had no luck at the mall, but they learned of an old shack used as a teenagers' hangout in the Southside Hills. The three men investigated this shack in the woods but found nothing.

Tulk was disappointed. "We went back to the police station, around 11:00 P.M. and I remember overhearing a plainclothes policeman tell another officer that 'This is bigger, different than usual.'" Even at that early stage of the game, the police were leery.

Throughout the week, the principal stayed in close contact with the police and kept the staff fully aware of any developments.

ON THURDAY, the St. John's dailies again ran Dana's photo and the story of her disappearance. *The Daily News* seemed to take a more active, campaigning role in the hunt for Dana Bradley.

The Daily News gave many personal details of Dana's life and family. "The young girl who mysteriously disappeared in St.

John's Monday ... is still missing." Dana's grandfather, Otto Bradley, had shown *The Daily News* his willingness to pay a reward for information leading to her whereabouts.

Det. Lloyd Ford told *The Daily News* that about ten officers were working on this case and several private citizens were volunteering in the search. He also pointed out that the Constabulary got many missing-persons reports, "but this one we're treating a lot more seriously than the rest."

THE DAILY NEWS echoed the high level of concern on the part of the RNC. William R. Callahan was the publisher of the paper, and lived in the area where the girl went missing from, and took on a crusading role in the Bradley case. Callahan believed the Dana Bradley disappearance was so important that it deserved more than just cursory news coverage. As publisher, he thought the abduction of this helpless young girl demanded special media attention.

The Callahan residence was on Cowan Avenue, which intersected Topsail Road, slightly west of the intersection where Dana Bradley was picked up. Currie Place, where Dana had been visiting her friend Penny Cobb, was also west of this intersection.

Bill Callahan's children, who knew Dana but did not go to school with her, were shocked to learn the news. "Our crowd knew her and were aghast when they heard the news. It caused great concern because it could have been one of our children. We had three girls. After that, every time they went out the door you were nervous," he says. There was a fear that the perpetrator would return and strike again. Parents in the area became very aware and concerned.

"We moved to Cowan Avenue in the 1960s," Callahan says. "There were very few homes. There was no Village Mall, no car lots, it was all farmland with a few barns. Then the neighbourhood started to grow fast. Schools like Beaconsfield were built. At the time every family on the street had kids. This was a busy, active, young neighbourhood." That there were so many youngsters in the neighbourhood led to some tension over the missing girl.

Because Dana was known to his sons and daughters, Bill Callahan felt keenly aware of the case. "It's appalling. It boggles the mind to think a young girl could walk down the street and vanish," he says.

Jim Thoms was the editor of *The Daily News* in 1981, and Bill Callahan remembers that Thoms also lived in the general vicinity, on Brookfield Road. "Most people at *The Daily News* had families, so it hit close on that level."

School Principal Fred Tulk also lived in the Cowan Heights area. So did RCMP Inspector Jack Lavers, who when events turned a dark corner would later lead the investigation.

Callahan at times felt as if the efforts of *The Daily News* weren't always appreciated. "I had the impression that some people in authority thought we were trying to create mass hysteria and panic. This wasn't the case. A very serious thing had happened in the community ... we felt the paper had a purpose, and we stuck our necks out many times. This one occasion demanded it."

In the rival newspaper, *The Evening Telegram*, RNC Det. Ford stated that police were receiving "a lot of calls, but nothing is checking out." The article reiterated Dana's description, the circumstances surrounding her disappearance, and that the police were very concerned for her safety.

By this time, Dana's family, friends, and teachers were positively frantic. After the first couple of days, Fred Tulk realized there was something more to this than a simple runaway. "My main concern was that she had been hitchhiking. I started warning the other students about the dangers of [it] in the week Dana was missing."

There was a common thought that no one goes missing in Newfoundland. No one wanted to believe it. A student at I.J. Samson recalls that "crazy rumours came up, like Dana was pregnant and ran away from home." These rumours weren't true of course, but they circulated on account of Dana's mysterious disappearance, in the way wild, groundless rumours surface concerning many things. And in a bizarre twist, "some weirdos showed up at the school making indecent proposals to the students."

All week long, students listlessly hung around the school entrances and on the grounds in small groups to discuss what might have happened to their friend. Dana was on everybody's mind. A popular, smart, artistic, well-rounded young girl does not just vanish. Where was she?

Four

AS THE SUN ROSE on Friday, December 18, Dana Bradley's disappearance had passed its fourth night.

Once again, the local papers ran stories about the girl's disappearance. "Dana Bradley of 160 Patrick Street is missing for the fourth straight day."

Det. Ford of the Royal Newfoundland Constabulary informed the press that he had nothing new to report on Dana's whereabouts and he issued another plea to the public for assistance.

Across town, *The Daily News* took the Dana Bradley story to a new level as it issued a "Special Appeal" to "some unknown person in the St. John's area who knows where Dana Bradley is."

> "There's a mother in St. John's suffering the terrible agony and anguish of not knowing what happened to her daughter only 14 years old.

But someone, somewhere in this area, knows where she is and what happened to her.

We are asking that someone to end the suspense, the agony, the not knowing of this situation by disclosing the whereabouts of the girl.

We know this person may not want to phone the police or Dana's home with such information, for fear that the phones may be tapped.

We can give assurance that the phone at *The Daily News* is not tapped.

There would be no thought of trying to trace the call.

We are arranging this appeal in full cooperation with Dana's mother and the police.

We ask only to be informed anonymously of Dana's whereabouts so that we can tell the police and they can end this agonizing suspense for the girl's family."

While *The Daily News* did not receive a phone call in response to its "Special Appeal," an answer to the riddle of Dana Bradley's whereabouts was soon to be revealed.

IT WAS NOW a week before Christmas, and in the afternoon, Helen and Dale Smith of Shea Heights, St. John's, loaded their children in the car and went in search of a Christmas tree.

It was cool and overcast, and while the temperature was above zero, high winds amplified the cold air blowing over the nearby Atlantic Ocean.

The family began driving out Blackhead Road heading towards Cape Spear, the most easterly point of land in North America, and a popular tourist destination, with its spectacular cliffs, pounding surf and sentinel lighthouse.

Leaving the community of Shea Heights and heading toward Cape Spear, the road begins to rise. The Smiths passed Beaver Pond on their right and crested a steep hill. As the road began to dip downhill and turn slightly to the left, they approached an intersection. Away to the left, across a large wooded valley, lay the rolling Atlantic Ocean. Dale put on his direction indicator, slowed down, and turned right onto Maddox Cove Road.

The Smiths drove half a mile along the road, passed a gravel pit on the left-hand side, and parked on the shoulder. The family began walking along a wooded trail, angling uphill.

At three o'clock, Dale Smith stumbled on the lifeless body of Dana Bradley. Mercifully, he had wandered away from his family, so his children were spared the frightening scene.

Smith told a reporter, "I went walking off to the left and I saw ... well, at first I thought it was a mannequin. All I saw were her legs. She was wearing jeans and she was lying on her back. I went back and told my wife. I never looked at her face, but my wife did, and she recognized her as the girl who was missing. We ran into another fellow who was cutting wood and he stayed with the body. We took our children back to the car, and we went back [home] together. I called 911 and the police came right away."

In short order, three unmarked police cruisers were at Dale Smith's house. The first police officers to respond to Dale Smith's call were members of the Royal Newfoundland Constabulary. He led them to Maddox Cove Road, and the police sealed off the area immediately.

When the call came into the police headquarters, "the police station just emptied," Jeff Levitz told *W5*. By approximately 3:30 P.M., officers had the area cordoned off.

A large contingent of police officers from both the Constabulary and the RCMP, accompanied by tracking dogs, immediately moved into the area. Since Maddox Cove was, at the time, outside the policing jurisdiction of the Constabulary, the RCMP assumed control of the body-recovery site and the investigation.

In a bizarre coincidence, Dawn Bradley was at the police station when Dale Smith's call came in. "They didn't say anything to me. I just knew," she said. "I went out back to where my car was and followed them [but] I got stuck behind another car at a red light. The police went right on through and I lost them, so I went home and called Jeff. I could see the police cars going up the road through my window. When Jeff came, we got in the car again and went in the same direction, driving around until we found them."

Access to Maddox Cove Road was up over the Southside Hills, readily visible from Patrick Street where Dana and her family lived. It was only twenty minutes away, so close and yet an eternity away.

At the scene, Dawn Bradley approached a police officer and asked him if the body was that of a girl. The officer instructed Mrs. Bradley to return to her car ... somebody would be with her soon.

Dawn and Jeff were advised that indeed, a girl's body had been found; that was all anyone would tell them. But the couple knew it was Dana. They returned to Patrick Street, where a number of people had gathered. Dawn Bradley's biggest concern at this time was her mother's reaction to the news.

The discovery of Dana Bradley's body sent shock waves reeling through St. John's and all of Newfoundland.

Five

THE AREA ALONG Maddox Cove Road where Dana's body was discovered is a remote, unpopulated, wooded region on the fringe of St. John's, approximately 14 kilometres from the downtown area.

Dana Bradley's body was located near an open area, sheltered with grass and alder bushes. The remains were found to the right of a dirt roadway leading into a field, which was approximately 30 feet from Maddox Cove Road. The area was well known to local people who frequented the Shea Heights-Maddox Cove-Petty Harbour area. Roadblocks were set up on Maddox Cove Road and no other persons or vehicles were permitted through the area.

ONE OF THE POLICE OFFICERS on the scene that afternoon was RCMP Inspector Jack Lavers. At the time, Lavers was

Assistant Commanding Officer for the St. John's Subdivision, and in that post he was responsible for investigating major crimes in the area. Lavers was at work that Friday afternoon when the call came in.

"Dana was not missing from our jurisdiction; she was missing from the Constabulary jurisdiction, so beyond having notice of her as a missing person, we had no involvement in the investigation. We only became involved when her body was discovered," Lavers recalls.

Pat Doyle had been a reporter with *The Evening Telegram* for 15 years in 1981. He came by journalism honestly, as his father was Gerald S. Doyle of the "Doyle News Bulletin." Pat was in *The Telegram* newsroom on Duckworth Street when the call came in that there was a flurry of police activity on Maddox Cove Road.

"I was on general assignment that day and it was late in the day when we got the call. I don't know how many people would have been left in the newsroom then. I think I was getting ready to go home for the day. You're the reporter that's on duty, you get the call, and you go. I think the word we got was that they found a body; we probably didn't know at that point that it was definitely Dana Bradley. Myself and photographer Dick Green drove up, and they had the road blocked off."

It was near dark by the time the veteran reporter and photographer arrived at the intersection of Blackhead Road and Maddox Cove Road. Doyle doesn't recall having any particular problems at the roadblock. If the police didn't know all the newspaper reporters, they did know the photographers, so identifying themselves as media wasn't a problem.

"We couldn't get very close because the road was blocked," Doyle recalls, "and Dick decided he would go up through the woods to see how close he could get to get a picture. I stayed with the car in case anybody came out, but I don't think Dick got very close. The authorities had it cordoned off. Basically, it was a case of waiting around. I wrote (the news story) on what we got from the police, which wasn't very much at that time."

Because it was late in the afternoon, just a few days before the winter solstice, police brought in large spotlights to illuminate the scene where Dana's lifeless young body lay. They remained on the scene throughout the night, searching for clues.

Mr. Doyle recalls that night as cold and dark, but it was dry since no rain had fallen. "It was not too bad a night in terms of weather for that time of the year," he said.

He and Dick Green stayed at the scene for some time, so long that Pat started to worry about his diabetes. "Earlier that year I had found out I was a diabetic, and for the first year I wasn't on insulin. When we got the call we took off and I didn't have anything to eat with me. I was getting a little bit anxious, because we were up there for a good number of hours. I might have been starting to get a little bit shaky by the time we got back to the office."

Because the discovery of Dana Bradley's body was such important news, and it was late when Pat wrote the story, the presses were held up to include the front-page news from Maddox Cove Road.

At times, as many as eight or ten police vehicles were at the site. Around 7:00 P.M. an ambulance arrived at the scene and the body was quickly taken away. A statement issued jointly by the

RNC and the RCMP stated that an autopsy was to be performed at 9:00 A.M. Saturday morning. The cause of death was not immediately known, but it did not appear to be of natural causes.

A special team made up of both Constabulary and RCMP officers was established to investigate the case. The RCMP took on the primary responsibility for the case, and because of his position, the task of supervising this investigation fell to Inspector Jack Lavers.

AROUND THE SAME TIME that Dick Green and Pat Doyle had left *The Telegram* office on Duckworth Street and began heading for Maddox Cove Road, Glenda Cluett was strolling up Water Street. Glenda had stayed off school that day because she was upset that Dana hadn't been heard from all week.

"I was partly thinking that I was the reason she had taken off. I guess I was feeling a bit bad," she recalls. "I was walking up Water Street passing by the old London store and the Musical Clock, and I met John 'Bull' Cook. He knew me and knew that I taught at I.J.Samson, and he knew Dana's mother. He said to me, 'They've found Dana Bradley.' I at once thought that was great, and I asked where she had been, and then he told me, 'She's dead.' I went into hysterics. I went into Sweetn's and phoned a co-worker."

At the same time that Dana's body was discovered and the area cordoned off by police, her classmates at I.J. Samson were preparing to go to the school's Christmas dance. Fred Tulk remembers the evening Dana's body was found.

Because he had been in contact with the police throughout the week, the authorities had promised to call the principal as soon as they learned anything about Dana's whereabouts.

"I got the call from the police that they had found her. I wanted to cancel the dance out of respect, but they said to go ahead with it. Then it was reported on the suppertime TV news that Dana's body had been located. So as I was going into the school to unlock the doors for the dance, the kids who were waiting around outside who had heard or seen the news were asking me questions as I walked by them."

The school normally held four dances a year, and the teaching staff took turns, splitting into four groups to act as chaperones. For this occasion, however, all the teaching staff were contacted and naturally, everyone who could, attended to lend support to the shocked youngsters.

Some teachers thought the dance was a way for students to get together and talk through the events, to grieve and perhaps begin the long road to healing over the loss of their smiling classmate. Besides staff, many parents showed up to chaperone. "I think going ahead with the dance was a good thing to help the kids deal with it. Most of these children had never had to handle death before and they were there with their friends," one teacher said.

Glenda Cluett avoided the dance altogether. She was simply unable to attend. The tragedy devastated her emotionally. "I was pretty upset that night. I was frantic."

A friend of Dana "thought the dance should have been cancelled, because Dana was missing and the theory was that something serious had happened to her. It was there at the dance that I found out Dana was dead."

"When the doors opened and the dance started, the kids were sitting in small groups here and there, in the corner of the gym, or in a hallway," the principal said. The dance was upsetting for everyone, and the sombre atmosphere inhibited the grief-stricken students. Nobody danced. Today, if such a tragic event were to happen, a crisis response team of trained counsellors is available to help students and staff deal with the loss. Unfortunately, in 1981 no such crisis management team or trauma unit was in place at the school board.

Given the circumstances, Fred Tulk felt that the teachers and the parents did their utmost to handle the situation. Trying to cope with Dana's death and help the distraught classmates was very tough on the teachers. "You try to carry on as normal as you can under the circumstances, but it's impossible. You just try and get through it. The other children became afraid, especially when they learned that Dana had been murdered."

Students and close friends were especially traumatized. One of Dana's friends was so deeply affected by the news that she slept with her bed flat on the floor for three years. Her father had to remove the legs so that it rested directly on the floor, since she was convinced a man would come out from underneath it. Each night, before she went to bed, her father checked the closet to reassure her nobody was in the room.

Some the teachers on the staff of I.J. Samson refuse to talk about it today because it is just too painful to go back over all those bad memories.

Six

JACK LAVERS HAD JOINED the Mounties in 1955, and he had worked on several murder cases over his years of policing. Dana Bradley was not the first murder victim he saw, nor was she the first young person he had seen murdered. However, the way in which the body was displayed was like nothing he had seen before.

Dana was found fully dressed in her school clothes, laid out straight on the ground on a slope overlooking Maddox Cove Road, with her feet pointing towards the road. Her arms were neatly folded across her chest and her school books tucked under one of her arms. There was no sign of struggle and no marks on the body, however, her left jaw was broken.

None of the details describing the way Dana's body was found were released to either the public or the media for many years. The police were playing their cards close to their chests to protect information that only someone who had been at the scene would have known. The way in which her body was found was anything but typical.

Jack Lavers: "The way her body was laid out in the woods was unique, in the sense that usually the killer has no respect or regard for the victim, and usually the body is dumped in the woods or in a ditch ... not laid as carefully as this body was laid out, with her books replaced under her arms. It indicated to me and other investigators that there was some level of remorse on the part of the person who put her there."

IN A MEDIA INTERVIEW years later, RCMP Corporal Randy Hogg said, "Usually, at most murder scenes someone is killed and found in a garbage dump ... or thrown out over an embankment or whatever, and any belongings are just thrown helter-skelter."

Dana Bradley was the only murder victim he had found laid out so carefully and, "I personally think that the person who did it probably had some sort of feelings for her, and didn't want her found just dumped by the side of the road. He wanted her to be found, and put [the body] in such a way that he thought it wasn't degrading to her."

There was no evidence to substantiate the murder had taken place at the site where the body was discovered, "but obviously the girl was not murdered in the position in which she was found," Corporal Hogg said.

Unfortunately, there was little evidence to assist police in determining where the crime had taken place.

RCMP Cst. Christine MacNaughton, a sixteen year veteran of the force is currently one of the lead investigating officers on the Bradley file. "The person responsible for this crime displayed the body in a manner in which she probably looked when he first met her, holding her school books. It's also a sign of how she would have looked when laid out for burial."

Given a sense of the killer having some element of remorse, it was reasonable for police to speculate that the killer was known by Dana.

"WE NEVER DID HAVE any indication that they knew her," Jack Lavers says, "but we were conscious of the fact a very high percentage of murders in Canada are done by people who know the victim ... maybe upwards of ninety per cent. Either relatives, a boyfriend, friend, a business acquaintance.

"So that's one of the first areas you look to when you go to investigate a murder, is whether someone with a relationship to the person was responsible. They're the first people you begin to eliminate as suspects," Lavers continued. "All her family and all her school friends were eliminated [as suspects] in the early stages of the investigation."

Surprising, it seems, several females were questioned during the investigation. "You have to think about that for a minute. It could be a female as an accomplice to a male, or it could be a female acting alone. I think they were both investigated. There were some very violent females around the town at the time who had an interest in young girls. So we received information about them, and of course we had to investigate."

There was no way of knowing whether Dana had put up a fight. Defensive wounds are ordinarily associated with knife attacks, but this murder appeared to be the result of a blunt instrument.

Lavers' gut reaction to whether the crime was committed by one person acting alone, or by more than one, was based on experience. "You go back to your best-evidence rule. You go back to the information we had at the time, and all the information we had from witnesses who saw Dana get into the car was that there was one person in the car. So there was never any indication there was more than one person ... but you can't close your mind to the possibility that person didn't take her to a spot where there was another person involved at some point in time. You have to be open to all the possibilities as you go through the process."

It was possible for one person to have put Dana's body where it was found. Jack Lavers: "Yes, it certainly would be possible. She was a young girl, not fully mature. Where her body was found was not that far from the road. The distance escapes me, but it was over the ditch and into the brush just a short ways from the side of the road. There was no indication there was any effort on the part of the person or persons who put her there to bury her or conceal the body. There was no debris, or brush, or rocks or grass or any effort made to conceal the body. For instance, there was a fender, or a hood of a vehicle very close to where the body was found, and there was no effort made to cover the body up with this large piece of metal."

Investigators believed that it was possible that Dana's body remained on the hillside for the four days she was missing. Exposure to the fluctuating weather, varying from sun, rain, snow, with high winds and temperatures above and below zero, would have hampered investigators' efforts to glean evidence from the body recovery site.

DR. ELLIOTT LEYTON is a well-known criminologist and the author of several books on murder. He has studied this phenomenon for many years and has been a consultant to several police forces around the world, including Scotland Yard, the FBI and Interpol.

When asked about what he inferred about the way the body was laid out, Dr. Leyton replied that there was "possibly some respect relationship, or possibly regret, remorse, or maybe just good old psychopathic obsessive/compulsion."

Whether there were other cases in which the victim was laid out so neatly, he replied, "Yes, this is not at all uncommon."

Seven

ON SATURDAY MORNING, *The Evening Telegram* carried the horrible news: MISSING GIRL FOUND DEAD.

The story was accompanied by a picture of the police roadblock on Maddox Cove Road, and readers learned how Dana Bradley's body had been recovered. A joint task force of RCMP and Constabulary members had been established, however, the cause of death was not yet known and was pending an autopsy report. More information would be released when more facts became available.

Ironically, *The Daily News* carried a short story titled, STILL NO LEADS ON MISSING GIRL. The morning newspaper had gone to press sometime before Dana's body was discovered.

NEITHER *THE EVENING TELEGRAM* nor *The Daily News* published on Sunday, but the next day, December 21, the awful truth hit newsstands and landed on people's kitchen's tables.

DANA BRADLEY DIES OF A BLOW(S) ... TO THE HEAD, screamed *The Daily News* headline.

GIRL DIED FROM BLOW TO THE HEAD; POLICE SEARCHING FOR MAN IN HIS MID-20S *The Evening Telegram* reported.

The heinous crime was now being intensively investigated by an RCMP-RNC task force numbering twenty officials: seventeen Mounties and three detectives from the Constabulary's Criminal Investigation Division (CID): The team was headed up by Inspector Jack Lavers and operated from the RCMP headquarters in Pleasantville. The RNC detectives working on the case were Lloyd Ford, Reg Meadus, and Calvin Rowe.

The autopsy performed on Saturday morning revealed "that death resulted from a skull fracture caused by what appears to be a blow or blows to the head by a blunt instrument. Death would appear to have followed the injury almost immediately."

At the time, Inspector Lavers refused to comment to the media whether or not Dana Bradley had been raped or sexually assaulted. He said further comments regarding the autopsy results at this time "could prejudice the investigation." Lavers told *The Daily News* that the time of death could not be precisely established, "but the death is consistent with the date of the disappearance."

Eight

ON MONDAY, DECEMBER 14, Harry and John Smeaton had been selling Christmas trees less than seventy feet from Topsail Road, out of a vacant lot across the road from McDonald's restaurant. Little did they realize they were about to become eyewitnesses in a murder investigation.

It was "getting kind of dark and quite cold," Harry recalls, "cold enough for us to be sitting in the truck."

The Smeatons were selling a few trees, "but it was our first and last year at it. Sales were not near what we expected. We were sitting in the truck commenting on people passing by, and we commented on this little girl who was hitchhiking."

To Harry, at first it seemed like the little girl was waiting around for the bus, but if she was, "she was not there very long when she put her thumb out and started hitching."

"We commented how foolish it was, a little girl hitchhiking," Harry Smeaton recalls. "Then a car pulled up and she walked over to it. The passenger door appeared not to open, and the driver leaned across and opened it for her. Then he drove off. We might've commented on the dilapidation of the car, and also that the girl was young to be getting into a car with a stranger."

The brothers sat there hoping to sell a few more Christmas trees and didn't give much more thought to the young hitchhiker they'd seen.

Not only did the Smeaton brothers get a good look at the automobile Dana boarded, they got a reasonably good look at the driver, given the distance they were from the car, and despite the fact in December it is dark by 5:20 P.M. A nearby street light helped provide some illumination.

Because Dana couldn't open the passenger door from the outside, the driver had to lean across the car and open the door for her. As the door swung open, the Smeatons looked into the face of the man who was in all probability, Dana Bradley's killer.

The RNC had been contacted on Wednesday, the day her photo and missing persons notice appeared in the local papers, but the Smeatons weren't contacted until sometime after her body was found on Friday. Now it had become a joint RCMP-RNC task force murder file. "A fair bit of time elapsed before we were called by the authorities. We were kind of ticked that it took so long for someone to get back to us. The week she was missing, no one called us."

Harry Smeaton was shocked when he heard the news that the missing girl was dead. "We didn't expect she'd show up dead. Probably we thought she'd been kidnapped, but I don't think we entertained the idea she'd turn up dead."

The Smeatons' recollections would later help the police put together the following portrait of the driver. He was described as being a clean-shaven man in his mid-twenties, of average height and weight, with light-brown, medium-length, unkempt hair. Based on this description, the Royal Newfoundland Constabulary and the RCMP released an artist's composite of what the man may have looked like.

This sketch, along with a picture representing the suspect car was first released to the public on Monday, December 21, a week after she went missing.

The Christmas tree vendors had become the key witnesses in what would eventually become one of the biggest police manhunts in Canadian history.

The Smeaton brothers were interviewed on several occasions, and police were convinced their accounts were accurate. Hypnosis strengthened the veracity of the information, as did another witness. A truck driver passing by also noticed the car stopped in the driving lane near the bus stop. This witness saw a young girl matching Dana's description run up to the car and lean in, talking to the driver. His description of the car corroborated that of the Smeatons. If he hadn't come along, or if the Smeatons had left their Christmas tree lot to go home for supper, Dana Bradley's death might have been a much bigger mystery. The statements may not have been much, but it was all the police really had to go on.

THE TASK FORCE asked for public assistance and got it in large measure. Hundreds of new tips poured in as Jack Lavers and the team went about interviewing and eliminating suspects.

One of the first things investigators checked was whether or not a suspect had a vehicle, or *had access* to a vehicle that fit the description of the car Dana was seen entering. Next, officers questioned suspects to determine their whereabouts on the evening of December 14 and whether it was believable and could be substantiated. Officers then took hair samples and checked these against hair found at the scene where Dana's body was discovered.

If suspects failed any of these tests, they were asked to take a lie detector, or polygraph test.

At the time, the RCMP and RNC did not have the benefit of recent advances in DNA testing, and this was a hindrance for the task force and Jack Lavers. "Hair is probably the least conclusive of all the physical evidence you can have available to you, in the sense that over time hair will change texture, colour. Your hair today will be different than your hair tomorrow depending on what you eat, how long you stay out in the sun. At that point all our lab could do for us was really tell us [whether or not] the hair was similar."

WHILE POLICE MAY NOT have gleaned much physical evidence from the location where Dana's body was discovered, they did have the Smeatons' description of the car and driver.

Harry Smeaton and his brother had it down to either a Dodge Dart or a Plymouth Valiant, yellow or pale green. "The car got tossed around in our minds in conversation. It was hard to give a definitive model. There was no definite ... I hassled it over with my brother over the days," Smeaton said.

The police were searching for a four-door, light-coloured Dart or Valiant with rust along the lower body. Both makes were very similar to one another, and fell into the 1973-1976 model range. It was hoped that if investigators could find the car, it might contain evidence which would link the driver to the murder.

Unfortunately, the police soon discovered that there were thousands of such cars on the roads in St. John's. "We determined the witnesses had a partial license plate number and a good description of the vehicle," Lavers recalls. "They were all in agreement as to the type, year, model, make of the vehicle, with a little difference in terms of how people saw the colour, whether it was beige or light green. Given the overhead street lights and the time of day, you could understand that."

In tracing vehicles through the Motor Vehicle Registry of the Provincial Government, many cars were found fitting the suspect car description. Complicating matters, files at Motor Vehicle Registration were incomplete. Some Dodge Darts were registered simply as Dodges, while some Plymouth Valiants were likewise registered only as Plymouths. This meant thousands of extra cars and records had to be searched.

Not only did police have to check vehicle records and then the actual cars, they also had to talk to the people who owned those vehicles and anyone who had access to them.

Officer Randy Hogg stated that when the RCMP began looking for the car, "it seemed like everybody had one, and it seemed like every single one had rust along the bottom. We've searched in excess of two thousand vehicles and we've never come across a vehicle that has any evidentiary value."

However, Hogg also stated that at times the RCMP thought they had located the car. On one occasion, a vehicle was found in such a hard-to-reach location that it had to be lifted out with a helicopter. "We've been through that car with a fine-tooth comb. We thought for sure we had the car, but we just couldn't find anything." Evidence like blood or hair would be hard to come by from a derelict auto that has been washed by rain, wind and snow for a long period.

Twenty-two years have passed since the disappearance and murder of Dana Bradley. Even if police located the car today, the chances are slim that it would provide any useful evidence to investigators. However, if the car had been kept in a garage over time and was protected from the elements, it might still contain useful evidence.

NOT LONG AFTER THE NEWS of the murder hit the streets, a rumour began to circulate that police had found a second body, or at least skeletal remains, in the general vicinity of where Dana Bradley's body was discovered.

It was thought that while the police were searching the Maddox Cove woods with a tracking dog, they had come across the remains of another missing girl who had disappeared without a trace in St. John's almost three years earlier. Inspector Jack Lavers flatly denied the rumours.

Somehow, it seems that the finding of Dana's body on the Maddox Cove Road gave rise to a distorted reference to an earlier missing person's bulletin.

Nine

ON MONDAY, DECEMBER 21, the same day that the suspect and vehicle descriptions were released to the public, Dana Nicole Bradley was laid to rest. The service was held at Wesley United Church on Patrick Street, just down the hill from where she had lived.

The school chaplain held an assembly at I.J. Samson school before the funeral service. Then the school was closed at noon out of respect for Dana.

"That morning was spent consoling the children," Fred Tulk remembers. "We tried to be as normal as we could in an abnormal situation. At this time, the childrens' feelings had changed from concern to fear. They'd become afraid for themselves, especially the girls. Some were crying, some were laughing, it was different the way they reacted to it."

The school emptied to attend the funeral and the church was packed with students and their parents, teachers, and the Bradley relatives.

The funeral service was a standing-room-only event. Dana's schoolmates sobbed hysterically in front of the casket placed before the altar, decorated for the Christmas season. The incongruity of the two events was startling: the horror and shock over the murder of an innocent, versus the happiness and love of Christmas.

Reporter Pat Doyle covered Dana's funeral and burial. "That was pretty hard, because all her classmates were there and they were crying and it was a bad scene ... and at the graveyard, too."

Rev. Robert H. Mills conducted the service, and his words expressed the outrage of the community. He also reflected on the fact that people tended not to think of such events happening here in St. John's, and held out the hope that Dana's death was not in vain, that parents and young adults would learn from the unfortunate events.

Dana's homeroom teacher, Glenda Cluett, was at the funeral. "Mrs. Bradley didn't go to the funeral, she was so upset. But it was blocked ... the students were all hysterical. Death is the last thing junior high-school students think about. They don't have any fear at this age, and they don't think about their own mortality."

From the church, Dana Bradley was carried to her final resting place in Mount Pleasant Cementery by six of her former classmates. Pictures of these young men carrying Dana's casket appeared in the papers, the grief on their young faces clearly visible. Standing in front of the Wesley Church on Patrick Street, the pallbearers could see the hills where her young body was found.

AFTER THE FUNERAL, Teacher Glenda Cluett and some of the girls who knew Dana went out to McDonald's restaurant. "These were mature-looking girls, pretty girls. They knew someone had taken Dana and killed her. At one time, these innocent young girls would have loved to have gotten a whistle from, say, a construction worker on the street. Now they told me they were uneasy with that kind of attention. Now they were scared and not comfortable with guys ogling them. They no longer saw this as frivolous; now it had a sinister side to it. That seemed kind of poignant to me. It was a turning point for them."

A child getting run down accidentally was one thing, but this was so different. Who had ever heard of a child getting murdered in Newfoundland? Dana's murder dampened the school spirit the rest of the year, and it affected some teachers their entire careers.

The students were in shock, intensified by the fact that I.J. Samson was such a tiny school, housing only grades seven, eight and nine. Every school year began with an assembly, motivating and welcoming students back into what the adminstration hoped would be an extended family. Now one of the extended family was gone, and it took a long time for students and faculty to adjust.

The day following the funeral, the school was scheduled to get their Christmas holidays, so the staff and students of I.J.

Samson had little time to reflect and to grieve as a community, before separating for the holidays

Glenda Cluett doesn't remember much about that last day of school. Principal Fred Tulk thinks that, all things considered, the Christmas break provided some space and time for individual students to grieve in the comfort of their families.

"When Christmas came there was a lot of guilt associated with it," a classmate of Dana's said. "This was survivor's guilt. I think the teachers might have felt this too. After Christmas everyone tried to make a fresh start."

For most people in ordinary circumstances, Christmas is a festive time that is looked forward to with anticipation. Rich foods, gifts, and gatherings of friends and family, make this a special time of the year, but for Dana's friends the holiday season had a dark cloud hanging over it. It was difficult to get excited about Christmas and all the things associated with it. People were torn by the opposing emotional forces tugging at them: immense sorrow and fear in a season of love and laughter.

Ten

IN THE DAYS RUNNING UP to Christmas, the Dana Bradley story dominated St. John's newspapers. Coverage of Dana's funeral service and the hunt for the killer were the main content of these items. Pictures of Dana's funeral shared space with pictures of the car police were searching for, and the composite sketch of the driver.

Jack Lavers and his investigators made a conscious choice to involve the community and the media in the case. "You very often get murder cases where police won't say anything about it. They go very private, almost introverted as far as the public is concerned, and say very little for fear of prejudicing the investigation. But we realized right up front a number of things.

"First, there didn't appear to be any connection between the perpetrator and the victim. "We had to rely on public input to give us information," Lavers stated.

As well, he believes it was only as the result of going public that investigators got the witnesses they did, such as the Smeatons at their Christmas tree stand. "It was because we gave it that broad public exposure that happened."

Another reason he decided to give the case such wide public exposure was related to the way Dana's body had been laid out. "Possibly there was remorse on the part of the perpetrator, and we wanted to use the time of year – the Christmas season – to maybe create a human situation, where the person who did it, if they were remorseful for doing it, might very well have come forward. That's why we gave it the public profile we did. That was a conscious plan on our part."

WHILE HIS INVESTIGATORS WORKED around the clock to apprehend the murderer, one can only imagine the heart-wrenching grief Dana's family and close friends were going through at this time. A few days before Christmas, the brightly coloured lights and pretty decorations did nothing to take their minds off the brutal killing.

A few years later, Dawn Bradley told *Newfoundland Lifestyle*, "If you're lucky enough not to crack up, then you've got to get through it."

The horrendous pain Dawn Bradley was feeling at the time would have been too much for many people to bear. However, a friend of hers told the magazine that "Dawn never went to pieces in public. She's extremely strong."

For the police detectives on the case, this also was a Christmas like no other. There was none of the last-minute rushing around to get gifts for their wives and children, no joyous, carefree, pre-Christmas parties. The investigators were like bloodhounds on the trail, relentlessly searching for the murderer who had stolen the joy from this merry season.

Policemen would find themselves spending the days before Christmas scrambling to crack a case in which the trail grew colder every day that went by, while the public's demands for resolution grew louder.

Jack Lavers: "I think you always do bring it home with you, in a case like that. We were so involved, and the community was so involved. The whole interest in the case was so high it did impact on everybody's life; not just mine, but everybody who was involved in the matter." All the people who worked on the case, especially in the early weeks of the investigation, made substantial sacrifices as they worked long hours and often got very little sleep.

Harry Smeaton sensed a frantic desperation on the faces of the police. "At the time, being involved with the officers, you could see they wanted to solve it. They were pretty involved emotionally. They were affected by this little girl taken the way she was."

THE EDITORIAL IN *THE DAILY NEWS* on December 22 was titled, GOD REST THEM. It eloquently captured in words the community outrage over Dana's senseless murder, and at the same time the massive outpouring of sympathy for the family.

> "There are occasions, rare occasions, when a whole community feels as one. So it is that the heartfelt sympathy of the people in St. John's and indeed in all of Newfoundland, goes out to the family of Dana Bradley."

The Daily News went on to say "Here is grief, agonizing grief ... that comes from the realization of a death for which there is really no plausible explanation. Except that some twisted mind against which there is no defense had to have his way no matter what the cost."

The editorial offered sympathy and prayers for the family. It stated how, despite parental guidance, sometimes the circumstances of life are such that things get put off course.

It also described the killer as a "fiend" with a "twisted, sadistic mind," and offered the theory that drugs were behind many crimes, suggesting perhaps that in this case, the murderer had his judgment hazed by mind-altering substances.

"We aren't anymore the safe quiet place we used to be." This accurately described the feeling that many people and parents felt subsequent to Dana Bradley's murder; that old St. John's was not as safe as they would like to believe.

The front page of the paper again showed a copy of the composite sketch of the suspect believed to be driving the pickup car. This was accompanied by a photo of a car similar to the make and model, for which the police were searching. Inspector Lavers told the media that no warrant had been issued, and because police were alert to the fact that the person being sought might try to leave the island, airports and ferry terminals were being watched.

If Dana were killed on the day she disappeared and brought to the Maddox Cove woods that same day, the killer or killers had a four-day window to hide the car, or clean it up and dispose of any evidence. Because officers were unaware for several days that a murder had even occurred, the culprit had a substantial head start over the police.

THE HUNT FOR DANA BRADLEY'S killer took on a new dimension when it was reported that the police investigators were now searching for a second man in connection with her death. "The special team of police investigators ... said this morning the man they are looking for is about 25 to 30 years old, with brown, bushy hair down over his ears. He also had a moustache and may be wearing tinted eye-glasses and a denim jacket."

Witnesses had come forward to the police and reported seeing a person matching this description in the Maddox Cove Road area the day before Dana's body was discovered. He had spent about two hours in the area, driving back and forth along the road in a green 1973 Chevrolet four-door sedan, similar to a Belair or Impala model. No other information was released, and the police did not say how this second man fitted into the investigative puzzle.

The news also reported that the police task force had received tips on many individuals and automobiles, and up to that point in time about fifty citizens and cars had been investigated, but Inspector Lavers told *The Telegram*, "We haven't arrested or questioned what we would feel to be a key suspect." He explained the police were going through a process of elimination, and that there was a great deal of information pouring in from members of the public who clearly wanted this case solved as much as the Bradley family did. The investigation was continuing at a swift pace.

Jack Lavers told *W5* later, "We (the investigators) had a great deal of information coming our way. We had a very accurate description of the vehicle. We had some description of a perpetrator seen leaving the scene. All of us were very confident that it would be solved, because we were solving all our murders here."

SUPPORTING THE SMEATONS' description of the car, another pair of witnesses came forward with an astounding story. A couple from Shea Heights were driving north along Maddox Cove Road around 11:30 P.M. on the night of Monday, December 14, when they came upon a car parked on the side of the road. The car was empty, but its passenger door was open and its dome light shone like a beacon, lighting up the beige interior. As they drove by the car, the couple caught sight of a man standing on the bank, ten to fifteen feet away. The man matched the description of the suspect as given by others. The police determined that he was standing at a spot very close to where Dana's body would eventually be located.

Was this man the killer, caught "red-handed" placing Dana's body in the woods, and did he get scared off before he had a chance to bury her?

Jack Lavers: "Well, I think the theory was that this person fit the description the Smeatons and others gave at the scene on Topsail Road. It was consistent with how they described the person and was also consistent with their description of the vehicle on Topsail Road at the pickup point.

"So we very much felt that this was the person coming out of the woods after the body was disposed of, because the people who came upon that vehicle saw the interior lights were on in the car and the right side door was open, which was next to the ditch, which was right in the immediate area where the body was found."

ON CHRISTMAS EVE, the local papers kept the case before the public. *The Daily News* reported again that police were still seeking two individuals in the death of Dana Bradley.

> "Police now say they are looking for two different men. One is the man seen picking the young girl up around 5:20 P.M. Monday ... near Tim Horton's on Topsail Road. The other man is said to have spent some two and a half hours in the vicinity where the body of the youth was found in Maddox Cove."

Investigation efforts had been stepped up, with additional RCMP members and Constabulary officers added to the task force.

Later that day, *The Evening Telegram* hit newsstands with a startling story. SUSPECT QUESTIONED, FREED FOLLOWING LIE DETECTOR TEST.

> "The special police team investigating the bludgeon-slaying of 14-year-old Dana Nicole Bradley of St. John's picked up a male resident of Kilbride yesterday for questioning but he was later released after taking a lie detector test ... The man also was the former owner of a car which resembled the vehicle the Bradley girl was last seen entering."

Insp. Jack Lavers told *The Telegram* the person from Kilbride had been picked up for questioning on Wednesday, after he had placed a notice in a newspaper advertising a car for sale. Suspiciously, the car fit the description of the vehicle authorites were trying to locate.

Initially the man in question couldn't satisfactorily explain who he sold the car to, but the police did find the vehicle and thoroughly checked it out. This person was thoroughly interrogated and voluntarily underwent a polygraph test, and was later released.

The police were still looking for the individual seen driving a Belair or Impala in the area the day before Dana Bradley's body was found.

Insp. Lavers also told the media that another witness had come forward who corroborated the eyewitness details obtained from the Smeatons. Lavers made it clear the police were still relying heavily on tips from the general public and were now involved in the time-consuming process of following up.

Eventually, investigators would identify two thousand vehicles that fit the description of the suspect car. Besides the confusion about how the vehicles' make and model were entered, the investigation was also hampered by the fact that in 1981, the province was in the process of shifting from a system of all-numeric licensing to a combined system of letters and numbers on license plates.

As if offering an explanation for why the special police task force had not yet caught the murderer, Lavers stated that computer readouts of motor vehicle registrations, lie detectors tests, and even hypnosis of witnesses had been employed. Though there was no evidence to suggest a sexual crime, known sex offenders were checked out. Nothing could be ruled out. A number of exhibits had been sent to the RCMP Crime Lab in Halifax, including plaster casts of tire tracks from the Maddox Cove area. "It's a painstaking process, as the team has to work without fingerprints or even a murder weapon."

Some of the officers working on this case had been getting only three or four hours sleep a day since the investigation started. However, all the efforts of this joint team of RCMP and RNC officers were unable to come up with an arrest and conviction. They would have liked nothing better than to catch the murderer. They were powerless to deliver the best Christmas gift possible to the family and friends, and to a worried public: the capture and subsequent conviction of the black-hearted criminal.

Eleven

While the joint team of investigators toiled throughout Christmas, they kept coming up empty-handed, despite the fact that media interest in the case remained high and the general public was continuing to submit many tips to police. Every scrap of information that came in had to be examined, meaning more work for investigators. The sheer volume of information illustrated the high level of public interest and support that grew out of a universal emotional response to Dana's murder.

The idea of giving the murder of the young girl such broad public exposure paid off. The tips rolled in. The phones rang off the hook. Everybody, it seemed, wanted Dana's killer caught.

Investigators interviewed nearly 250 persons of interest. This involved taking hair samples, polygraph tests, investigating backgrounds, checking alibis, and determining ownership or access to the suspect vehicle type.

With all of the vehicles identified in the motor registration division, owners and former owners had to be confirmed and investigated, as well as those who might have had access to them on December 14. Was the vehicle owned by her murderer, or borrowed from a friend or perhaps a landlord? Jack Lavers and his team had their work cut out for them. When the police viewed the motor vehicle records, it seemed that everybody had a Dodge Dart or Plymouth Valiant.

A WEEK AFTER DANA was buried, *The Evening Telegram* ran a front-page story that declared, ONE SUSPECT SOUGHT IN GIRL'S SLAYING. The investigation was now narrowed to focus in on one suspect and one vehicle. Further witnesses had come forward and their statements were being assessed. A day later, the media reported that the police had no new leads in the Bradley killing. New information was not ready to be released, since the police had not finished working with it.

Lavers, who was doing everything he could to crack this case, revealed that an RCMP specialist had been brought in from Ottawa's Criminal Identification Branch. Staff-Sgt. Pat Dunleavy was regarded as one of the top experts in the field of composite drawings in Canada. In fact, he had helped develop the system for identifying criminals with composite drawings that was being used by police forces across the country at the time.

Dunleavy planned to re-interview several witnesses and try to put together another drawing. If it were vastly different from the previous sketch, it would be released to the media, Lavers announced. The Christmas season posed some difficulties, since some witnesses had gone out of town for the holidays and had to be asked to return, otherwise the sketch analysis would be delayed.

There was a nagging, troublesome possibility. What if the suspect vehicle were dumped or hidden somewhere? If police couldn't identify a specific car currently in use, they would have to seriously consider the idea that it was dumped. The possible locations of where the car might have been discarded were numerous, and no investigation had yet been done along those lines.

Dana had gone missing on Monday the fourteenth, and was not found until Friday the eighteenth, and that entire week was very wet, with exceptionally heavy rainfalls, as if the heavens were crying for a missing angel.

The area where Dana's body was discovered was near a gravel pit off Maddox Cove Road, the kind of place young couples might go parking, or young fellows would go to have a beer. It was easily accessible, but tucked away and difficult to notice, especially if it is nighttime and the person is unfamiliar with the vicinity. She may have been murdered in the gravel pit, but more probably somewhere else. It seems unlikely that the young girl was killed at the spot where her remains were found because of the lack of physical evidence there.

Two weeks after Dana had gone missing, doubt was developing whether the killer would be caught. Journalist Jim Thoms gingerly hinted at the possibility that Dana's killer might elude capture.

Thoms's story was the first journalistic hint that this case might go unsolved, and surfaced in *The Daily News*, which had taken such an active campaigning role in the hunt for Dana's murderer. The staff at the paper were tired of reporting the empty results of the massive police dragnet.

Thoms wrote, "There's an air of quiet confidence among the policemen in St. John's who are looking for Dana Bradley's killer. Not that they will comment one way or the other on their chances of finding the man."

The authorities, Thoms added, were using "slow, methodical, plodding ... old-fashioned, non-glamorous police work that nearly always succeeds if success is possible."

Thoms was witnessing what he believed to be a murder case dragging on with no foreseeable conclusion. Though there was a large number of police on the case, they were coming up empty-handed. A massive volume of tips from the general public was coming in to the searchers, but the trail was growing colder. Jim Thoms voiced everyone's growing fear that with each passing day, the scent of the fox was growing fainter and the hounds were falling behind.

As time went on, the investigators realized Dana's murder was not going to be solved in short order. St. John's had experienced two or three murders a year up to that point, and they were usually solved fairly quickly.

Jim Thoms was also the first journalist to ask whether or not the defenseless teenager had been sexually assaulted. He pointed out that Insp. Jack Lavers had not said whether or not the autopsy report confirmed sexual assault, but Thoms noted "the family of the 14-year-old girl requested in her funeral notice that in lieu of flowers donations could be made to the Rape Crisis Centre in St. John's."

ON NEW YEAR'S EVE, Staff Sgt. Dunleavy's new composite drawing was released to the media and the public.

The alleged perpetrator's height was listed as five feet, seven inches, with a slim build and collar-length, dirty blond, or brown, unkempt hair. The man was thought to be 25-30 years old, and his eyes could be hazel-coloured.

This sketch varied from the earlier version in that it resembled a photo, and showed the suspect with longer, shaggier hair, a straighter nose and an almost fair, baby-faced complexion.

Harry Smeaton provided information for the new composite. "They brought in an expert from the Mainland with a kit of eyes and noses and chins. I was not real happy with the sketch. I spent so much time at it, trying to picture it in my mind and trying to get it out. And you had two people (Harry and his brother) looking at it."

Staff Sgt. Dunleavy's composite appeared to show the suspect likeness with a baby-like face, but this was not a nod towards a school-age suspect. "I don't think that beyond the first few days, any of Dana's friends were ever considered primary ongoing suspects," Jack Lavers says. "The composite that Dunleavy did was not a composite that in any way related to any of Dana's friends."

Composites can be misleading and not absolutely reliable. Jack Lavers: "If you take a composite from three different people, three people will see someone differently. If you can get a general appreciation from the composite, that's fine, but to say your composite is going to be a dead ringer, I don't think that very often turns out to be the case." When Dunleavy's composite was released to the media, it was stressed that the drawing was intended to be only a likeness and not an exact replica.

The Evening Telegram headline accompanying this new sketch was titled, SUSPECT KNOWS HE WAS SPOTTED. The new image of the suspect was also based on eyewitness testimony from the two witnesses on Maddox Cove Road the night Dana went missing.

Because the suspect knew he was seen, it is reasonable to conclude that he left the area immediately, or took steps to clean up the vehicle and other sources of evidence, or even dispose of the vehicle.

Police now expanded the colour of the car to include tan, faded yellow, beige, pea green, or lime green. The differences in colour was attributed to the way the car may have appeared under artificial street lighting on Topsail Road versus how it looked in car headlights on the darkened Maddox Cove Road. The car was also now described as having an antenna on its right fender.

Insp. Lavers told *The Daily News*, "The vehicle was seen on the Maddox Cove Road, parked immediately below where the body was found. The man was seen between the vehicle and the woods, and about 75 feet from where the body was found." Despite the December cold, the man was not wearing a jacket.

This couple, who wished to remain anonymous to the public, thought little of the man they had seen and continued their drive home. As far as they were concerned at the time, it could have been simply a case of the man relieving himself, or poaching game.

The task facing the investigators was daunting, because of the large number of cars in the St. John's area fitting the description of the suspect vehicle. It is a testament to the efficiency of the police that over 800 automobiles had been tracked down and examined between December 20 and December 31, an average of 72 cars per day over the eleven-day period. Included in that process, many innocent citizens were subjected to questioning by the police task force.

The public, however, was responding very patiently to the efforts made to apprehend the murderer. The police were "contacting the registered owners of something like 1,600 cars in the area and, they say, despite all the inconvenience resulting from this, they are getting excellent cooperation and assistance."

The writer of an editorial in *The Daily News* stated that "people in St. John's where the crime occurred are anxious that the guilty one is apprehended and brought to justice." The writer also described the murder as a "savage crime foreign to Newfoundland.

"We are certain that this spirit of cooperation and goodwill will continue for as long as the investigation lasts ... for this kind of attitude vastly improves the chances of a successful conclusion to it."

Twelve

NEW YEAR'S DAY in 1982 fell on a Friday, two full weeks after Dana Bradley's body had been discovered. These had been fourteen days of non-stop police work, a media blitz, and massive public assistance, and still no suspect was in hand.

The New Year started on the same note the old year had ended, an unresolved murder case dominating media coverage. On its first day of publishing in the New Year, *The Daily News* front page once again displayed the composite of the main suspect in the murder. Insp. Lavers said that as soon as the new composite hit the media, the calls had started coming into police. They had received about 100 calls, and they were still coming in.

The information was now more detailed and focused primarily on the drawing of the suspect. "As a result of the new tips submitted to the police, a number of individuals fitting the general description have been questioned and eliminated. No one has been placed in custody," *The Daily News* reported.

Insp. Lavers believed the killer was still in the general vicinity of St. John's, because "to leave the area would draw attention to himself." However, RCMP detachments throughout the province were on alert and were watching for anyone resembling the composite, or any vehicle matching the suspect auto.

Like a fox who runs from its raid of a henhouse back to the safety of its underground den, the criminal was riding out the storm of media coverage blanketing the St. John's area. The killer had done the job well. There was no murder weapon left where Dana's body was found. If the murderer were successful in cleaning the car of any blood or hair samples, or if the perpetrator had managed to drive the car over a cliff and into the ocean or into a deep pond, he might feel confident that he would elude capture.

On January 4, the media carried a short story titled, POLICE STILL SEARCHING FOR SUSPECT. This story was brief and carried very little new information, except to note that the second composite drawing "met with excellent response." It would take police some time to follow up on all the leads they received.

The brevity of the news item and the subdued title was indicative that the story was now beginning to get old, and was being supplanted with more current, fresh news. The failure of investigators to deliver a prime suspect quickly was wearing on everyone. While everyone wanted resolution, the days were slipping away and the cold days of January had arrived, with no fresh scent on the killer's trail. He had covered his tracks and now winter storms would slow down the search and conceal any evidence left to the elements.

While Dana's slaying was a massive personal crisis for Dawn Bradley, the murder had been transformed into a public loss as well. Dana had become everyone's daughter, everyone's friend. So many young girls who had hitchhiked could easily have been the victim.

In mid-January 1982, Dawn Bradley made her first public statement, one of the very few occasions on which she would do so. A month from the day Dana first went missing, *The Daily News* carried a statement from Dawn Bradley, thanking the public for their support and assistance, and thanking the police for their efforts in searching for the killer.

> "We would like to be able to personally thank everyone who has helped by prayers, company, phone calls, letters, cards, kindness and love, but it is impossible.
>
> We have received approximately 600 sympathy cards from friends, relatives and unknown friends from Port aux Basques to St. John's. Every day there are more and each one is appreciated. For whatever individual reasons this has reached the hearts of everyone in Newfoundland, and we are very grateful for your concern.
>
> There are no words to express our gratitude to the Royal Newfoundland Constabulary and the RCMP who believed in us and stayed by us those first four days, and did everything humanly possible that there was to be done and still doing so.
>
> A special thank you to Dana's friends, of which there were many, who only confirmed by

their concern and caring our knowledge of what
a beautiful person and daughter she really was.
Signed
Sincerely,
Dawn Bradley and Jeff Levitz for the
Bradley and Thomas Families"

Just as a false rumour circulated in December that a second body had been found in Maddox Cove, in January, another rumour circulated through St. John's that the police knew the identity of the killer. These rumours were so persistent that the investigative team issued a statement denying they knew the identity of the murderer.

In response to the massive number of tips and leads coming in, the police team grew to 30 officers, and by the end of January, to 35. For the first several weeks and months of the investigation, officers worked in teams of two, in order to handle the volume of information coming forward, and eliminating people as suspects. In Jim Thoms's words, the investigators were "literally snowed under by possible leads from a concerned public."

Near the end of January, a huge snowstorm hit St. John's. The ice-cold snow descended. The killer's trail was rendered invisible. With January and February historically the worst winter months in Newfoundland, snow and wind threatened to hamper efforts to locate the suspect car.

It was to be one of the worst winters experienced, and this seriously affected the search for the vehicle, crucial to forensic research. If the suspect had dumped the car on some woods road, or other out-of-the-way area, it was now buried under snowdrifts and was out of the reach of the investigators.

The weather presented a major hurdle to the investigators. "As we got further into the investigation, the weather played a major factor," recalls Jack Lavers. "That was probably one of the worst winters we ever had for snow and cold." Snow made it very difficult to establish a connection between the suspect and the vehicle. February brought with it vicious storms.

One of the worst hit on Friday, the fourteenth of February. This blizzard was severe, laced with extremely high winds. When the morning light broke on Saturday, February 15, the awful news was reported that the *Ocean Ranger*, the largest semi-submersible off-shore drilling rig in the world, was missing, with 84 crew presumed drowned, including 56 Newfoundlanders. This new tragedy now demanded the media's attention, and the unsolved murder was quickly overshadowed, but never completely forgotten.

Newspaper coverage in the unsolved murder waned as 1982 began to wear on. "I think that is probably accurate and probably understandable, in that other intervening factors in the news – like the *Ocean Ranger* disaster, which had a major impact on the community," Jack Lavers recalls. "We were working away during that period of time, but there was really nothing newsworthy to report that the media would be interested in. During all those first years, continual resources were being spent on the file ... human resources, time and money ... hypnotizing witnesses ... people who come forward with seances, psychologists."

In late February, 1982, Journalist Jim Thoms updated his readers. "Police have rejected for the time being the possibility of offering a reward for information leading to the arrest and conviction of Dana Bradley's killer ... But they are leaving it open for future consideration. They just haven't reached that kind of dead end in their investigation into the death of the St. John's teenager."

A reward had been considered on more than one occasion, but police always decided against it. The public response for assistance was remarkable and it was felt a reward would not be helpful.

Lavers flatly denied the police had reached a dead end in the murder case and told Thoms that, "We are still getting about a dozen calls a day ... We're doing all we can with just as many men involved as when the investigation started. We are not scaling down in the least ... There's every indication the team will stay in place ... because we have a lot to do."

Up to this point, police had questioned hundreds of people, but not all of these were necessarily suspects. They had also checked out most of the 1,600 vehicles in the model range identified. In addition, another 500 autos from the 1972 year model were examined. There were, however, some cars they just couldn't find. This may have been due to the blizzards and snowdrifts piling up, or because the investigation, as a murder case, started four days late. Dana had gone missing on the fourteenth of December, and the police had not been aware a murder had occurred until the eighteenth, when her body was found. Four days was plenty of time for the killer, with or without an accomplice, to discard the vehicle.

By March, the RCMP had widened its search for the murderer. Two cities the Mounties were reported to be searching were Toronto, Ontario, and Fort McMurray, Alberta. Both places were well-known destinations for Newfoundlanders looking for work.

Commenting on their efforts, Sgt. Harold Avery said the investigators "have no particular suspect in mind at the present time ... there are a lot of transient people in the area (Fort McMurray) and a lot of unsolved murders in the west. We are checking to see if there are any similarities or connection between cases out there and our own investigation." It was also disclosed that a team of investigators had been sent to Ontario to interview a person who went to that province shortly after the Bradley murder.

The police had widened the scope of the investigation into a nationwide search. Officers were sent across the country and into the United States, wherever the information led them, with no limits on manpower or budget.

Investigators were still checking out leads with respect to the vehicle, and Avery told *The Telegram* this was one of the most difficult parts of the investigation as "some of the cars are not so easy to locate, because they may have been sold to another person ... but by the process of elimination we will hopefully get a break."

In April, *The Evening Telegram* reported that the five members of the RNC who had worked full-time on the file had been transferred back to regular duties with the constabulary. These officers included: Det. Sgt. Cal Rowe; Det. Reg Meadus; Det. Lloyd Ford; Det. Bob Pearce; Cst. Melvin Cake.

This reassignment of duties coincided with the expanded geographic responsibilites awarded the RNC in policing areas like Newtown, Donovans, East Meadows, and Wedgewood

Park. As part of the expansion, over 40 new recruits were to be hired, and the five senior investigators were needed to help train them.

The constabulary officers' knowledge of the city had been an immense help to their colleagues, especially in the early stages of the investigation. Now only the RCMP remained on the file.

As the force caught up with the workload of checking out potential suspects, the staff numbers would be slowly reduced. Considering the amount of things to be handled, the Serious Crime Unit of the RCMP continued at full staff for quite a long time. Seventeen officers continued working on the case.

One of the most important tasks was the continual followup on numerous leads concerning the suspect vehicle. In mid-April both *The Daily News* and *The Telegram* ran stories dealing with the "car problems" the RCMP were having. Finding the particular car became more and more like looking for a needle in a haystack. At this time, there were still 350 remaining to be checked out.

While 1,600 cars had been investigated, a discrepancy in the motor vehicle registration system meant that almost 400 Darts and Valiants had been registered as just Dodges and Plymouths, requiring the Mounties to recheck all the records and cars.

The number of calls from the public were now slowing down, compared to the frenzy immediately following the murder, however, the Mounties were still receiving two to three calls a day.

Jack Lavers described the "car problems."

"As an investigator, you always have to take your best information and best evidence and go with what the witnesses are telling you ... Dodge Darts and Plymouth Valiants turned out to be the suspect vehicle, according to the witnesses. The witnesses had a partial license plate number and a good description of the vehicle. They were all in agreement as to the type, year, model and make of the vehicle, with a little difference in terms of how people saw the colour.

By early May 1982, the RCMP had checked almost two thousand cars and come up empty-handed. The nationwide search for Dana's killer saw suspects being questioned in Nova Scotia, New Brunswick, Quebec, Ontario, Manitoba, Alberta, and British Columbia.

Everyone was now wondering. Had Dana's killer, or killers, fled Newfoundland before her body was discovered?

IN DECEMBER OF 1982, a year after Dana Bradley was picked up and murdered, 25-year-old Henrietta Mille disappeared without a trace from a St. John's nightclub called The Key Club. Miss Mille was originally from Nain in Labrador, and was of Inuit descent. Her child was in foster care in outport Newfoundland, and Mille had apparently said or hinted she was going to hitchhike out around the bay to see the youngster.

On the night she was last seen, Miss Mille was having some trouble with a couple of patrons at The Key Club, but nobody could recall seeing her leave the premises, alone or with someone.

Mille's purse was picked up at the club. It contained all her personal information, such as banking material, keys, and an address book. Incredibly, the fact she was missing was not reported to police for several weeks later. Police used the date her purse was picked up as the date she went missing.

Three years before Dana Bradley had been killed, 17-year-old Sharon Drover of Livingstone Street in St. John's disappeared. She left home to pick up a paycheque at McDonald's on Kenmount Road during the last week of December and has not been seen since.

Janet Louvelle, of Corner Brook on Newfoundland's west coast, went missing February 6, 1979. Four months later, a wildlife conservation officer discovered her decomposed body near a woods road outside Corner Brook. The girl's clothing and belongings were scattered about the vicinity.

Sharon Drover, missing from December 1978; Janet Louvelle, in February 1979; Dana Bradley, murdered in December 1981; Henrietta Mille, missing in December 1982. Is it a coincidence that three of these four females went missing in December? Was a serial killer on the loose in quiet little Newfoundland?

Would the authorities ever catch Dana's killer?

Pictorial
Section

Dana Nicole Bradley

Dana Bradley attended I.J. Samson school the day she went missing.

Early police composite of a suspect

Subsequent police composite of a suspect

A Dodge Dart or Plymouth Valiant, similar to this was believed used in the murder.

Aerial view of the Maddox Cove Road body recovery site

Closeup of the Maddox Cove Road body recovery site

This girl is missing
and police are concerned

The Royal Newfoundland Constabulary says it is concerned for the safety of 14-year-old Dana Bradley of 160 Patrick St., in St. John's, who

Police are look

Missing girl found dead

By PAT DOYLE
Telegram Staff Writer

The body of Dana Bradley, a 14-year-old St. John's girl who had been missing since Monday afternoon, was found in a wooded area off the Maddox Cove Road, approximately three miles from the city, Friday afternoon.

A joint statement issued by the Royal

EVENING TELEGRAM – SATURDAY – DEC. 19, 1981

ty as her actions had not been those of a runaway, and she was known to hitchhike.

Her body was discovered at approximately 3 p.m., Friday, by a family from the general area who were searching through the wooded area for rabbits.

A large contingent of police officers from the Constabulary and the RCMP are

was still missing and had "developed a number of leads which have to be tracked down."

He added that they were then at the point of having to sift through a great deal of information and "the next 24 hours is going to be a pretty busy time." When that has been completed, he said, there may be sufficient information to indicate some

Dana Bradley died of
"a blow(s)... to the head"

By BREN HOGAN
of The Daily News
At this point in time

ficers and detectives from the criminal investigation division (CID) of the Royal Newfoundland Constabulary.

almost immediately," Insp. Lavers said.
He would not say whether the girl had been raped or

She had phoned her mother to advise that she was then leaving for her home at 160 Patrick Street.

Flood of tips on Bradley case
pouring into Crime Stoppers

A veritable flood of apparently new information is pouring in

a two-year prison sentence for obstructing justice. A stay of pro-

death of Dana Bradley.

Mount Pearl man charged in Dana Bradley's murder

The St. John's detachment of the RCMP has arrested a Mount Pearl man in connection with the 1981 murder of Dana Bradley.

Proceedings put on hold in Bradley murder case

The Crown has decided, following an intensive and costly police investigation into the December 1981 death of 14-

of Somerton's record which contain five prior offences, including robbery. Simmonds said Somerton hasn't been

| briefly |

Bradley murder case still open

The 10-year-old investigation into the murder of 14-year-old Dana Bradley is still an open file and new leads are investigated on an almost weekly basis, according to RCMP Inspector Larry Warren.

...her body was discovered, RCMP officers

Mounties' new techniques
may solve Bradley murder

The Dana Nicole Bradley murder mystery yet be solved by new improved techniques in t

John's, he said, adding that leads

Roberts reiterated Friday that appropriate to enforce the law."

Police still getting tips about Bradley's murder

Headlines from the Bradley case

Some missing persons cases. Pamela Asprey (top left) disappeared November 1984. Janet Louvelle (top right) went missing on February 6, 1979 and was found murdered. Marilyn Newman (bottom right) was found murdered January 1983. Sharon Drover (bottom left) has not been seen since December 1978. Henrietta Mille (not pictured) has been missing since December 1982.

Thirteen

From 1982 to early 1986, media coverage of the Bradley case diminished, even though the RCMP investigation continued. Things heated up considerably in January 1986, when a suspect was charged with first degree murder. Over the next few days, the Dana Bradley case once again dominated media coverage in the province.

ON TUESDAY, JANUARY 14, 1986, a banner headline announced MOUNT PEARL MAN CHARGED IN DANA BRADLEY'S DEATH. The story was accompanied by a photo of Dana, as well as a copy of the second composite that had been released to the media on December 31, 1981, and a picture representing the suspect vehicle.

The accused had been arrested at 6:00 P.M. the day before, and was scheduled to make his first court appearance the day the story broke in the media.

For the first appearance, the provincial court on the fourth floor of Atlantic Place in downtown St. John's was crowded with people waiting to get a glimpse of the suspected killer, David Grant Somerton.

Somerton was charged with first-degree murder. He made his court appearance amid tight security as plainclothes RCMP officers used the fire exits and back door to whisk the accused into and out of court. The media was prevented from getting any photographs or film of the accused, whose address was listed as 24A Jersey Avenue, Mount Pearl. Police taped paper over a window in the courtroom door to prevent cameras filming Somerton in court.

Members of the media and the general public were searched by the constabulary and court officials before they were allowed into the courtroom, where the accused was seated between two mounties. It was reported that up to ten RNC and RCMP officers were present in the courtroom, including Inspector Jack Lavers.

To compensate for the tight security in the courtroom, *The Telegram* ran a photo of Somerton's Mount Pearl residence. It was some time before David Somerton's photo actually appeared in the paper, however, it was able to provide a physical description: 35 years old, five feet, eight inches tall, with short, light-brown hair, a moustache and goatee.

The charge against Somerton was read by Judge John Trahey. It was alleged that on or about December 14, 1981, Somerton committed first-degree murder against Dana Bradley near Maddox Cove Road. Crown Prosecutor Colin Flynn asked to have Somerton remanded in custody until he could be interviewed by a psychiatrist. Judge John Trahey ordered that Somerton appear again in court on Thursday, January 16, at 2:00 P.M.

St. John's attorney Robert Simmonds acted as defense counsel for the accused. He requested an order prohibiting publication of any evidence presented in court; Judge Trahey accepted this request and granted a publication ban.

Immediately below the story about Somerton's first court appearance ran a short item that stated the accused had moved into the generally subdued neighbourhood in Mount Pearl, which included Jersey Avenue, where he occupied an apartment with a woman.

Neighbours reported that Somerton was quiet, kept to himself, and did not engage in much conversation with them. A media informant stated "He had no phone ... he sometimes asked if he could use our phone to call a taxi or whatever, and he had no car. He also asked other neighbours to use their phone, and even then he said very little."

THE FIRST TIME INVESTIGATORS had looked at David Somerton as a person of interest was sometime in December of 1981, shortly after Dana's body had been found.

"But we didn't look at Somerton in connection to a vehicle," Jack Lavers recalls. "The first time we looked at Somerton as a possible suspect was a very casual kind of contact, in that we determined at that point Somerton didn't have a vehicle or didn't appear to have access to a vehicle that matched the description of the suspect car we were looking for. We had further tips with respect to Somerton during January, and we went back to Somerton again in February. So he was a person of interest in the early stages of the investigation, but there were hundreds of such people, and Somerton in the first go-round didn't stand out any more than anybody else."

DAVID GRANT SOMERTON made his second court appearance as scheduled, however, even bigger news than this was now being reported. The Mounties had returned to Maddox Cove Road. The RCMP were preparing to go to war on the hillside, hunting for evidence that might have been buried there. Since Somerton had been charged with Dana's death, all the stops were being pulled to secure the evidence necessary to convict the accused.

The newspapers told a grim story. RCMP search teams were reported to be combing the area where the girl's body was found. Two large photos accompanied the story, one showing two RCMP members with picks and shovels getting ready to attack the frozen ground in search of evidence, and another startling image of an RCMP Staff Sgt. pouring gas into a chainsaw, readying to clear forest. The Mounties had become convinced there was evidence buried somewhere on this lonely, desolate hillside.

Staff Sgt. Penney led the search team of a dozen or so RCMP officers dispatched to the area. The Mounties had roped off an area 1,300 feet along the road and 125 feet back from the road. This area was then subdivided into 50-foot wide sections to be searched with a fine-tooth comb in the hopes of finding evidence related to the murder investigation. Officers employed everything from picks and shovels, to axes and chainsaws and metal detectors in their hunt. "We are looking for material evidence that might support a criminal investigation, that's all I can say," Staff Sgt. Penney told reporters.

Seventeen years after Staff Sgt. Penney made this statement, I talked with Jack Lavers about the search and what exactly the Mounties were looking for in the brush and woods off Maddox Cove Road. While being questioned by the RCMP, the accused had confessed to murdering Dana and hiding the murder weapon.

"He indicated to us where he buried the murder weapon on Maddox Cove Road," Lavers said.

I asked Lavers if he could tell me what type of weapon the accused had said was buried along the Maddox Cove Road.

"He (Somerton) said that he used a blackjack, which is a lead-weighted weapon on one end, with a spring handle."

If they could recover this weapon, it possibly could be used to successfully prosecute this five-year-old murder case.

AT HIS SECOND COURT APPEARANCE, David Grant Somerton was remanded to the Waterford Hospital for a 30-day psychiatric assessment to determine if he was fit to stand trial. Provincial Court Judge John Trahey ordered the 30-day assessment and scheduled Somerton to appear in court again mid-February.

Tight security measures had been repeated for Somerton's second court appearance, which was a relatively brief ten minutes. Somerton stood emotionless before Judge Trahey and a courtroom packed with Mounties, the media, and members of the general public. After the proceedings, he was whisked out a back door.

The RCMP also expanded their digging and shifting work from Maddox Cove Road to the St. John's city dump. While David Grant Somerton was undergoing a psychiatric exam at the Waterford Hospital, the officers were now beginning to excavate a section of the city dump where up to 300 cars were buried under tons of concrete debris from the demolished Hotel Newfoundland. The RCMP staked out a section of the dump where abandoned cars had been buried, a practice that ended four years earlier.

The Robin Hood Bay sanitary landfill site was opened in 1963 after the old landfill on Empire Avenue was closed. In the first 25 years of operation, there was little restriction on the type of waste that could be disposed of.

In 1981 a person could just go in and dump car wrecks, at the time considered garbage. It was years later that a municipal policy resulted in the establishment of a metal recycling company near the landfill.

During the 1986 excavation at the city landfill, the Mounties refused to say if they were looking for a car, saying only that they were looking for evidence in relation to Dana Bradley's death. However, *The Telegram* quoted an anonymous source to suggest the police were looking for a 1976 blue Ford car. The newspaper reporter speculated on the hard job the Mounties faced.

> "If they are looking for a car it will be a daunting task. Not only are the cars buried

under tons of rubble, many of them were burned in accidental fires before they were buried.

Most of the cars buried there were abandoned by their owners, who frequently removed any serial numbers so the cars couldn't be traced."

Jack Lavers recounts from memory: "He (Somerton) indicated to us that he took the vehicle he was using and put it in the dump."

IN MID-FEBRUARY, following his first and second court appearances, Somerton appeared in court before Judge Joseph Woodrow, who remanded him in custody until later in the month, to determine if there were enough evidence to proceed with the first-degree murder charge. A publication ban on evidence in place during the pre-trial court appearances would remain in effect. Defense attorney Robert Simmonds consented to Somerton being remanded until the twenty-eighth and waived the accused's right to appear before a judge every eight days.

About a week prior to the appearance before Judge Woodrow, Somerton had appeared in court and made a bail application, which had been denied by Madame Justice Margaret Cameron. The bail application hearing was closed to the media and the public, so the reasons for Justice Cameron's decision were not known. It was known that the psychiatric assessment had been completed, and Somerton was deemed mentally fit to stand trial.

RCMP teams were still searching the dump and the Maddox Cove Road areas, and Crown Prosecutor John Byrne said he hoped to be able to inform the court on February 28 when the investigation would be completed and when a preliminary inquiry could start.

IN JANUARY 1986, after four long years of hunting and searching across the breadth of North America, it seemed like the RCMP had finally solved the Dana Bradley case. If they could just come up with the vehicle and the murder weapon to support the charge, a successful prosecution would practically be guaranteed.

Jack Lavers discussed the decision to lay charges and conduct the search on Maddox Cove Road and the St. John's landfill site.

"Those of us heading up the investigation had to make a choice, of whether you're going to open the door and let him go and conduct the investigation, or whether you're going to lay charges and conduct the investigation. Of course, in the circumstances we didn't feel we could release him. We felt he had to be arrested, charged, and remanded in custody to give us sufficient time to see if we could find the things he said were there."

IN THE FIRST FEW MONTHS of 1986, the Newfoundland general public was left to wonder how the RCMP had come to the decision to charge David Somerton with Dana Bradley's murder. Very little information was made public, as a court ban was in place.

How did it come about that David Somerton came to be arrested and charged with the murder of young Dana Bradley?

"There was a note found in the post office mailbox in-box," Jack Lavers recalls. "It was a handwritten note on lined paper that indicated the author of the note knew who the person responsible for Dana's murder was, and the person responsible was Somerton. So we dispatched teams to investigate.

"From the note, we were able to raise numbers that had been written on a page above the page that the note had been written on. And the numbers were prescription numbers. We then took the prescription numbers and went to the pharmaceutical association. They were able to tell us what drugstore to go to, who the prescription was in the name of and what it was for. The prescription was in the name of David Somerton."

At this point, investigators still didn't know who had written the note, but they did know where Somerton lived.

"When investigators went to the house," Lavers said, "they found a pad of paper that the note had come from and were able to raise from the paper left on the pad, parts of the note. Eventually, handwriting comparisons established that it was Somerton who wrote the note, but he admitted to writing the note during the interrogation process."

However, the first-degree murder charge had not been laid against David Somerton solely on the basis of this note.

"No, no. He subsequently was arrested and admitted writing the note, and he made a confession, and then as a result of his confession the charge was laid. A team of two senior investigators did the interrogation, and I observed most of the interrogation through a one-way glass. He (Somerton) was quite convincing in the fact he gave a statement that he was able to describe how he killed Dana Bradley, what weapon he used, where he did it, how he did it and when he did it. And, there were certain things within his statement that we had not released to the public and we didn't expect that he would know.

"I don't want to get into what Somerton said in his confession because he is still a person of interest to the RCMP, and his confession might very well at some point have to be resurfaced. I have to respect the ongoing investigation as it exists now."

There was a sense of relief among the police when, after four years, they had a suspect in hand. "During that whole period of time, it was very much a roller-coaster kind of experience," Lavers recalls. "He wasn't the first really prime suspect that we came up with; there had been others before. And, there were any number of absolutely weird things that happened during that period of years."

For example, in the initial stages of the investigation, the police were delayed and thrown off the killer's trail by a man who was picking up young girls in the Topsail Road area at that time.

"Initially, when we started the investigation, several of these girls came forward and identified what turned out to be the wrong person. It took us about three to four days to apprehend that person. We found out that the person was not the real one that we were looking for, but he was active in picking up young girls in that particular part of town. So there was some delay and confusion in terms of composite drawings and things of that nature."

Another suspect the police investigators had to deal with was Bruce Gerard Connors. Shortly after Dana's body was discovered, Connors began making prank calls to the Bradley home, often late in the evening. Sometimes he would cruelly ask for Dana, while on other occasions he said, "I killed Dana."

"From people calling the Bradley home and saying they were the one responsible for the murder, and us then having to get telephone taps and chase them down – this wasn't the first situation we had to face," Lavers said.

Since Connors had to be traced and apprehended, this process directed valuable resources away from the real killer's trail and diverted the attention of detectives. Connors was ruled out as a suspect and was given a nine-month jail sentence for public mischief. However, for Jack Lavers, the RCMP investigators and the Bradley family, the roller-coaster ride had only just begun.

Fourteen

In 1986, public expectations of a conviction were quickly dashed. After a meeting in the office of the Minister of Justice, government announced, "The Crown has decided, following a costly and intensive police investigation into the December 1981 death of 14-year-old Dana Bradley to place a stay of proceedings on a first-degree murder charge against David Grant Somerton, charged three months ago in connection with the teenager's death."

"AT SOME POINT DURING that process (of searching the dump and digging near Maddox Cove Road) he changed his story," Jack Lavers said. "He (Somerton) denied that he had done this and recanted his statement. We couldn't find the physical evidence, so we felt at some point down the road, a month or two later when he was coming up again for trial, we didn't have enough for a conviction. So rather than go forward with the trial and, it would appear, have a dismissal, we thought it would be more prudent to stay the charge and continue to investigate. Because once he's tried and acquitted he can't be tried again."

A stay of proceedings did not mean the charge had been dropped or that the accused had been found not guilty. A stay of proceedings puts the charge on hold for one year, during which time the accused may be brought to court again to face the charge.

When the stay of proceedings was entered, Bernard Coffey acted as Crown Prosecutor, and Robert Simmonds as Somerton's defense. Details of the case were now released that had not been previously made public.

Coffey stated that while being questioned by RCMP Cpl. Randy Hogg, Somerton confessed he had abandoned a Ford automobile at the city dump, and that he had buried a blackjack near where Dana Bradley's body was discovered.

Within a week of being charged, David Somerton told his lawyer that the information he gave was not true. Lawyer Robert Simmonds passed this information on to the Crown.

Coffey stated that about $600,000 had been spent on the two searches, plus "a considerable utilization of police manpower." The investigation was still ongoing.

The Crown Prosecutor asked Judge Joseph Woodrow to impose a heavy sentence on David Somerton and pointed out the maximum jail term for such an offense was 10 years.

Defense Counsel Simmonds countered that obstruction of justice charges are normally laid against a person or persons trying to avoid responsibility. However, in this case, the court was faced with a situation where the accused had brought attention to himself by leaving a note at a post office which implicated him in Bradley's murder.

Simmonds told the court that Somerton's implicating himself in one of the highest-profile murder cases in the province was "a stupid act." He didn't think his client realized what he was doing.

Simmonds also told the court David Somerton had a very unfortunate background and had spent many years in foster homes. In recent years he had suffered from family and marital problems. Somerton was said to be undergoing psychiatric counselling for his problems, and Simmonds suggested to the court that these problems, combined with a sad family background, probably led him to implicate himself in Bradley's death. No one can fully explain why Somerton made statements to the police which implicated himself, Simmonds said.

The defense attorney also told the court his client had told him the statements about the car and blackjack were not true, and that he had not killed Bradley.

Crown Prosecutor Bernard Coffey presented Somerton's police record sheet to the court. It revealed Somerton had five prior offenses, including robbery. Simmonds countered by saying Somerton hadn't been in trouble for six years, and since his last conviction, had made "valiant efforts toward rehabilitation," had gotten married, and had children.

No murder weapon had been found buried near Maddox Cove Road, nor could the police find the car in the St. John's city dump. After many hours had been pumped into the search, and after huge sums of money had been spent, it appeared to the investigators that no physical evidence could be found.

After hearing the facts of the case, Judge Woodrow commended the police on their efforts in seeking out any clues in the case. He imposed a two-year sentence on Somerton for obstruction of justice, and explained this sentence took into account the fact that Somerton had been in police custody since January 13, almost four months.

FIVE CHRISTMAS SEASONS had passed since Dana was murdered. The highly publicized police searches of Maddox Cove and the city dump had been like a dam burst, a blessed relief. If the general public had heaved a collective sigh when David Somerton was first charged with murder, any sense of closure was dashed when the stay was entered and the searches of Maddox Cove Road and the city dump turned up no evidence.

The renewed public scrutiny of the case forced the Bradley family to relive the terrible events. Another New Year had started with Dana Bradley's murder dominating news coverage throughout the province. Newspapers, radio and television had given top billing to the arrest of David Somerton.

Because of his interest in the case, Bill Callahan remembers well the period in which a suspect was first charged with Dana's murder. "The Police seemed to keep indicating they knew who did it, then Somerton came along. They always seemed on the verge and edge of laying a charge and getting a conviction. But nothing came of it."

MORE THAN TWENTY YEARS after he implicated himself in the Dana Bradley murder case and served two years for obstructing justice, David Somerton talked with CTV's *W5*. He said that when he was first approached for questioning by the RCMP around the time of Dana's death, he had just gotten out of Springhill Federal Prison in Nova Scotia, after serving six years for armed robbery.

He told W5 that after being in the RCMP interrogation room for eighteen hours, he was in a suicidal state and was "on the verge of flipping out."

When asked what he thought he would gain by confessing to killing Bradley, Somerton said, "To be honest with you, I don't know. There's so much going on, being said down there, and seeing snakes crawling around the grass and rats crawling around you."

He told the RCMP to charge him or get him out of the room. "And then I started telling them where, where the car was. And I told them where the murder weapon was." In the television documentary, David Somerton stated that he confessed to the murder and fabricated false leads to get the RCMP off his back and free himself from that interrogation room.

In the years after he served his term for misleading the Dana Bradley murder investigators, David Somerton again found himself in trouble with the law. In 1996 he was convicted of indecent assault involving a teenage girl. He failed to appear in court for a sentencing hearing and was arrested on a Canada-wide warrant, at which time he pled guilty.

Somerton was asked point-blank by W5 if he had killed Dana Bradley. "I most certainly did not," he replied. He also said he didn't know who killed the girl, but if he did he would tell the police.

RCMP Constable Christine MacNaughton informed W5 that David Somerton "has not ever been fully eliminated as a person of interest in this file."

SOMETIME AFTER BILL CALLAHAN joined *The Evening Telegram* in 1987 as Managing Editor, David Somerton came into the newspaper office to discuss matters related to his part in the whole Bradley drama.

"I can't remember who instigated the meeting, whether it was the paper or Mr. Somerton. I don't remember the circumstances. But I recall we interviewed him in the boardroom, and I remember him saying the day would come when it would come out."

Fifteen

IN 1989, ON THE EIGHTH anniversary of Dana's murder, *Newfoundland Lifestyle* magazine ran a lengthy story outlining the course of the Bradley murder investigation to that point. As part of this special, there was an interview with Dana's mother, Dawn Bradley Levitz. It was rare for Dawn Bradley to speak with the print media about what had happened to her daughter and her feelings on the matter. The interview was a revealing glimpse into the life of Dana's mother. This case had been in the public eye for eight years, and still new information was being released to the public. It was like an onion being peeled, and this was another, deeper layer, closer to the true core of the Dana Bradley story.

Also interviewed with Dawn was her good friend Judy Price, described as "a constant support during the ordeal that followed Dana's disappearance." Dawn disclosed how she had had a feeling something terrible had happened to Dana when she was late returning home; how, despite reassurances from the police, she was convinced her daughter had met with foul play.

Dana's mother had kept her feelings to herself and close family. She didn't attend Dana's funeral. "At the time, I thought she should have been there," Judy Price said. "I didn't realize, but I do now. Dawn responded very privately – she didn't ever go to pieces in public. She's so extremely strong."

Dawn told the magazine she had no regrets about her relationship with her daughter, and added they had a close loving relationship, more like sisters than mother and daughter. The article also revealed a most difficult outcome of the murder. Dawn Bradley found that people were uncomfortable mentioning her daughter's name for fear of upsetting her. Judy Price, however, "... would go there and we would talk about her. She would say her name – Dana."

Dawn was strong enough to deal with the recurring public interest in the case, which peaked each December, and was prepared for the media coverage that time of the year.

IN 1990, IF SHE WERE still alive, Dana would now be 23, out of high school and perhaps would have started a successful career. These were nine years of freedom for the killer, scorning the police and mocking the justice system.

In October, two skeletons were discovered in the St. John's area. One was found in the Shea Heights area, the other off Kenmount Road. Initially, speculation was the remains might be those of either Sharon Drover, Henrietta Mille, or Pamela Asprey, all of whom went missing from around the same time

Dana was murdered. However, the two skeletons both turned out to be male. The remains in Shea Heights were those of a 50-year-old man who had been reported missing 18 months earlier. The other male skeleton was not identified.

The discovery of the remains in the Shea Heights area, near Maddox Cove restarted the roller-coaster ride of emotions for authorities, the media, and the Bradley family.

Constable Bill Dwyer was working on the Bradley file at the time. He told the media the RCMP believed they knew who the killer was, but had to be very careful because they did not have sufficient evidence to proceed to court. Cst. Dwyer also confirmed the public was still calling the police with tips.

Dana's killer was described as the "number one prize catch" for the B Division of the RCMP in Newfoundland.

IN MARCH, 1991, A RE-ENACTMENT of Dana's disappearance and murder was aired on television and sparked new leads for investigators. The four-part NTV special announced a $10,000 reward offered to anyone providing information leading to the arrest and conviction of Dana's killer.

As it was from the start of this murder case, public input was driving the investigation, and because of the lack of physical evidence, the RCMP were still relying very much on the support and help of the general public. The television special generated about 200 calls to police.

In December, the RCMP still had forty suspects under investigation, narrowed down from 1,800 suspects since the investigation started. Ten years after her brutal slaying, the Newfoundland public was assured the examination of Dana's death was still very much a priority for the Mounties and that they would continue to search for the killer until they got their man. Though the RCMP were doing their best, their reassurances were no longer convincing. However, the fact so many leads and calls poured into police after the television special aired was a testament to the diligence of the people of Newfoundland.

BY THE END OF 1992, the hunt for Dana's killer took a new twist when the newly established Crime Stoppers program began publicizing the case. This organization publicized a 1-800 number at which citizens could anonomously leave tips for the authorities. On December 4, 1992, Dana Bradley's murder was featured as its unsolved crime of the week. The report gave an overview of Dana's disappearance, murder, subsequent police hunt for the killer, and offered a $1000 reward for any information leading to the arrest of the person responsible for the crime.

The Newfoundland public refused to let her memory die. This crime would not go unsolved. Citizens cried out for action and pushed the police to hunt for the murderer. Just four days after the reward was offered, the Telegram reported a "veritable flood of apparently new information is pouring in to Crime Stoppers concerning the Dana Bradley case, raising hopes that the killer will yet be found and punished."

As a result of the Crime Stoppers publication, no fewer than 30 tips had been received from as far away as Port aux Basques. RCMP officer Cst. Rod Kavanagh, who was coordinating *Crime Stoppers*, reported that some of the tips could have a bearing on previously given alibis and vehicle ownership. In addition, one person from Port aux Basques gave $1000 to supplement the $1000 offered by Crime Stoppers.

A year later, in December of 1993, still with no closure on the Bradley file, St. John's again had two newspapers in production. *The Daily News* had closed shop, but *The Telegram* was still pushing copy off the presses daily, and a new weekly, *The Express*, was now providing a news service to the greater St. John's area.

Twelve years to the day Dana's body was discovered, on December 18, 1993, *The Telegram* reported "police still getting tips about Bradley's murder." RCMP Cst. June Ramsay was one of the investigators on the file. She told the paper "this file will never be closed until such time as we charge the person responsible." Tips were still coming in, especially during the month of December.

Across town, the weekly tabloid, *The Express*, carried a similar story, although there was a less positive tone to this piece. Cst. Ramsay told the paper she was hopeful the crime would one day be solved, but that it was becoming more difficult as each day passed. A huge obstacle facing authorities was time, during which witnesses forget details of events that were more than a decade old.

Now the field of suspects was narrowed to three individuals. While the RCMP had previously travelled throughout Canada to question suspects and/or witnesses, the recent tasking of five Alberta RCMP officers to the Bradley file foreshadowed a whole new twist in the investigation. The search for Dana's murderer was about to heat up again in the rolling foothills of oil-rich Alberta.

Sixteen

IN EARLY FEBRUARY 1994, the RCMP were hot on the trail of a prime suspect, a former Newfoundlander living in Alberta's wild rose country. Under the headline RCMP PROBE NEW CLUES IN DANA BRADLEY MURDER, Editor Gary Dimmock confidently predicted that "The RCMP are on the verge of cracking the most notorious slaying in Newfoundland history, after questioning four key witnesses and a prime suspect – all now living in Alberta."

The primary suspect and three of the four others being questioned were all former Newfoundland residents now residing in the oil patch.

As the murder investigation heated up, the media coverage intensified, feeding the public's fascination with the most well-known unsolved crime in the Island's history. Now, the Mounties were working simultaneously in both Alberta and

Newfoundland following new information that had come forward during the fall of 1993. The anonymous hotline of Crime Stoppers seemed to be paying early dividends.

The chief investigator on the Bradley file was now RCMP Sgt. Keith McGuire, and he had travelled to Edmonton for nine days in December 1993 to interview a male suspect. This particular suspect was questioned on three separate occasions by McGuire and other officers from Alberta's Major Crimes Unit. Besides the five RCMP officers in Alberta working full-time on the investigation, there were three Mounties from Newfoundland.

Sgt. McGuire stressed to the media the questioning of the suspect was more than just a routine interrogation. "I would say they are key witnesses – I can't confirm that they witnessed the murder – but it's good information ... the people were relevant." McGuire also publicly confirmed the main person of interest in Alberta was considered a very strong suspect by the RCMP.

The possibility of an Alberta connection to the murder made front page news in Newfoundland. In a tightly woven story, Journalist Craig Jackson contributed to the rising suspense in this new turn in the Bradley drama.

Sgt. McGuire stated the suspect in Alberta was well aware he was under investigation. He told *The Telegram* the RCMP had "received this person's name back in the fall of 1992 as a suspect in the case ... it was relevant to go and interview him in Alberta." The Sgt. refused to confirm if the male suspect who was interrogated or any of the four witnesses were natives of St. John's.

"I can't say that we're confident that we're going to make an arrest, and I can't say that we're confident that this is going to be solved," Sgt. McGuire said. "At some time, I'd say that some-body will have to make a decision on what we can do with that information, but for right now we're just continuing to investi-gate the homicide."

McGuire said DNA (deoxyribonucleic acid) testing of sam-ples from the case of Dana Bradley had not been done up to that point, and he would not reveal if the RCMP intended to use this powerful investigative tool. DNA is the genetic blueprint of a cell, and no two persons have the same DNA, except for iden-tical twins.

EDMONTON IS A NEATLY LAID OUT, sprawling modern city. The streets and roads extend whip-straight and intersect at regular intervals, city blocks are square, and a sense of sym-metry abounds. Traffic speeds along on highways through the heart of the city. There is no oceanic influence here, no rain, drizzle or fog.

It's a long way from Edmonton to Casey Street in St. John's. Casey Street is in the heart of St. John's, the oldest city in North America. Here city streets twist and turn, following the ancient paths they once were. Casey Street is close enough to the har-bour for residents to smell the salt water, and is located just one street east of Patrick Street, where Dana Bradley lived in 1981. Both streets run down over the same hill toward the har-bourfront area. From either street, one can watch the fog creep in over the Southside Hills, the rolling hills that stretch towards Maddox Cove.

In March of 1994, the RCMP intensified their efforts and conducted a search on the Casey Street residence of David

Grant Somerton. When this was reported in the media, Sgt. McGuire refused to comment specifically as to what the Mounties were looking for. "Basically, any dealings we have with private citizens is private information between us and them, which I can't make public. That's under the Privacy Act."

McGuire did say the RCMP had "an ongoing investigation relative to the Dana Bradley homicide and some of it does involve, well, obviously, things in St. John's. That's the only comment I have."

Four days after the initial media notice of the search on Casey Street, *The Express* ran four stories related to the ongoing Bradley murder investigation. Like *The Daily News* in the early weeks of the hunt for Dana's killer, *The Express* took an active, almost inflammatory role in the renewed search for the murderer.

RCMP PROBE MURDER SUSPECT'S HOME, read the headline on page 3. It was reported the search of David Somerton's rented apartment at 73 Casey Street occurred on March 30 and was led by Sgt. McGuire.

> "The search warrant, issued the same day (March 30), stated there was reason to believe that photographs, documents, newspaper articles, polygraph and DNA testing information related to the 12-year-old homicide were inside the small Casey Street apartment."

A second story was titled POLICE TO QUESTION COUPLE. Apparently, *The Express* had learned the Shea Heights couple who spotted a man coming out of the woods on Maddox Cove

Road on the night of December 14, 1981 was about to be questioned again by the RCMP.

The Express carried two more stories related to the Bradley case. One of them concerned David Somerton specifically. He was now claiming that in early January he underwent a series of lie detector tests administered by the police at a city hotel. Mr. Somerton stayed in one unit, the police in the adjacent unit. After the polygraph tests, RCMP officers drove Somerton to the site where Dana's body was found on Maddox Cove Road.

Somerton claimed police had taken a blood sample from him for DNA testing, collected in his kitchen before two police officers and five other witnesses. He also agreed to undergo a personality test consisting of over 100 questions.

Around the same time a blood sample was being taken from David Somerton, RCMP officers in Alberta were also collecting hair and blood samples from a resident in that province who had been interrogated in December of 1993. This person was less than 30 years old and worked at an Alberta printing company. The DNA samples were collected from the suspect at RCMP headquarters in Edmonton, and the young man also underwent a polygraph test.

For the first time, the RCMP confirmed that "foreign scalp and pubic hair were found at the scene." This public admission exposed another layer of the onion, revealing a deeper level of information about the repulsive homicide.

Since investigations were ongoing simultaneously at opposite ends of the country, it was not surprising that *The Express* reported "police believe more than one assailant acted in the 12-year-old murder." This echoes back to the week following the discovery of the murder victim. At that time, the *Telegram* had reported, "police are now searching for a second man," but a week later were back to focusing on one suspect only.

Now, years later, police apparently were again searching for two suspects.

The day following this intense coverage by *The Express,* David Somerton held a press conference at his home on Casey Street.

"Charge me or get off my back," Somerton told *The Telegram.* He was tired of being harassed by the RCMP and denied any involvement in Dana Bradley's death. At the press conference, it was revealed that on January 6 that year, the RCMP had taken Somerton to the Battery Hotel for polygraph tests. Three lie detector tests were given over the following couple of days.

"They said the results of the polygraph tests were inconclusive, but they told me I can't see the results unless I am charged," Somerton told *The Telegram.*

After the tests, Somerton said, he was taken to the site where Dana's body was found. He said this was the first time he had ever been there and that he never knew the girl.

Somerton informed the media that the RCMP search warrant was with his lawyer, Greg Stack, and that the warrant stated the RCMP believed he was responsible for Bradley's death. He stated, "they (RCMP) are under pressure to make an arrest and they are trying to pin it on me. But I don't think they are any closer to making an arrest than they were 12 years ago."

David Somerton claimed that when he initially confessed to murder in 1986, he was under a lot of pressure and using alcohol and drugs. He said he was placed in a small room in RCMP headquarters in Pleasantville and questioned for hours. While he was told he could leave at any time, he said the door to the room was locked.

"I got fed up with it all and finally said, 'Yes, I did it, now you prove it' Then it will be my turn, because I will be taking legal action as soon as all of this is over."

AFTER MONTHS OF TENSE DRAMA, cross-country questioning, and house searches, Sgt. McGuire announced to the public in June, "we're going to ask for approval to lay charges." An information package on the investigation would soon be forwarded to RCMP headquarters and the Provincial Justice Department with a request to lay charges. McGuire also confirmed the person questioned in Edmonton, Alberta was still a suspect.

At the end of June, 1994, police were back in court to secure an extension to hold items received in the search of the Somerton residence on Casey Street in March. The items taken included booklets used in a law course relating to violence against women, information on DNA analysis, newspaper clippings, photos of Somerton in 1981, and pictures of vehicles.

Responding to questioning by Somerton's lawyer, Sgt. McGuire admitted Somerton was a suspect and explained that retaining photos was crucial to the investigation in that they showed how David Somerton looked around the time of Dana's murder in 1981.

Judge Robert Smith presided over the application, and after listening to arguments by Stack and Crown Prosecutor Wayne

Gorman, ordered the police to return the booklets and newspaper clippings to Somerton. However, he granted a six-month extension for police to retain the seized photos.

Somerton told *The Telegram* he was expecting to be charged with murder, but maintained his innocence. "I know in my own heart and soul that I did not kill Dana Bradley, and I'm willing to go to court to prove myself innocent if I have to." Somerton didn't have to go to court in 1994 to prove his innocence. Nor did he have to present his case the following year; no charges were laid.

In early 1995, a news headline said it all: JUST ONE COP ON BRADLEY CASE; DNA TESTS INCONCLUSIVE SO FAR. The investigation had slowed to a crawl once more. The storm of police activity and media scrutiny subsided. Another New Year had started, and Dana's killer was still at large.

Seventeen

DESPITE THE NERVOUS anticipation and media hype in 1994, no charges had been laid in connection with Dana's murder and no killer brought to justice. In March of 1995, a story broke that using computer technology, police had generated a profile on the murderer. Would this new approach result in a conviction, or was it grasping at straws by investigators left high and dry by a cunning killer?

Information describing all the known circumstances around the murder had been entered into a new national database called ViCLAS, or the Violent Crime Linkage Analysis System. This system was adopted from an American model and was developed as a result of several multi-jurisdictional killings in the 1980s, like the infamous Clifford Olsen murders.

This new computer model allowed investigators to very quickly compare a murder with other such crimes across the country. It was based on the idea that serial killers operated with the same behaviour, even across hundreds of miles.

It was not known if Dana Bradley had been murdered by a serial killer, or if it were a random act of violence, so the police had entered the details into this computerized network. Dana's case had involved DNA testing, and now it was applied to this new criminological assessment tool.

Meanwhile, Crown Prosecutor Colin Flynn had asked the court for an extension of the length of time police could hold photos seized from the Somerton residence. His request was reviewed, and Mr. Justice Keith Mercer granted the Crown an extenstion of 18 months, but stipulated police must turn over copies to Mr. Somerton. This was the fourth extension granted to the RCMP by the courts to hold the Somerton photos.

The Crown application to the courts stated the RCMP investigation had intensified in the past 24 months and was nearing an end. This development, coupled with the request to hold the Somerton photos may have given the impression charges would soon be laid, either against Somerton, or some other suspect in Alberta. However, no charges resulted from the recently stepped-up RCMP investigation. The rapid progress which seemed to have taken the Mounties to the brink of apprehending the guilty party stalled once more.

IN JUNE, IT WAS REVEALED that the RCMP were working on a major report on the murder. There was some hint an arrest might result from this document, however the RCMP were being cautious in discussing the case and the likelihood of charges. Upon submitting the report, the legal staff would decide whether there was adequate evidence to proceed.

RCMP Supt. Gary Duff disclosed there were several suspects in the case and the RCMP needed legal advice from the Justice Department to determine if they had sufficient grounds to proceed. Up to that time, there were no results from DNA testing of crime-scene materials that had been carried out earlier in the year at a lab in Boston, Massachusetts.

As far as the media was concerned, the Bradley case was again beginning to grow cold. There were no startling new developments, no imminent convictions, no horrible new details, except that the whole cast of characters was back in court, this time before Judge Joseph Woodrow. The Crown was seeking another extension on its right to hold items seized from Somerton's residence. This application by the Crown dealt with different items than the previous extension that had been granted in March by Justice Mercer.

Colin Flynn informed the court of the items it wanted to retain, through RCMP Cst. David Esbary, who explained, "... one is a blue denim billfold that was taken from his wife, Connie. It has a photo of David Somerton taped to it." The Constable explained to the Court this photo was significant in terms of the investigation because it showed how David Somerton looked during the early 1980s when Dana Bradley was murdered.

In this Crown application, Flynn also asked for permission to hold files concerning David Somerton the police had confiscated. One was a file of the Somerton family, from the Director of Youth Corrections, as well as hospital records in connection with Somerton's brother, Trevor Somerton. According to authorities, Trevor Somerton was relevant to the case because "he is also one of the individuals of concern in this investigation."

The public was now getting a glimpse into the investigation from late 1993 to mid-1995. In addition, Somerton was becoming more of a public figure in the whole case. Now the public learned of more intimate details of his life, his family, the fact a file had been kept at Youth Corrections, and the name of another person of interest in the case, Trevor Somerton.

As with other details in this murder case, the glimpses were brief and revealed only a little each time. The family and public were again left in limbo, without an arrest and conviction that could bring closure. We only have snippets of insight into how this whole process impacted on Dana's relatives, especially her mother and stepfather. Jeff Levitz made comments to CTV's *W5* which provide a little insight into how difficult this never-ending process of police investigation and media hype was on the Bradley family.

"You'd see him (Somerton) around the odd time, you know, and how do you deal with that? I don't think that we were, you know, you're going to go out and shoot the guy because you think he got away with it ... because you really didn't know whether or not he did do the crime."

The comments made by Jeff Levitz alluded to a troublesome reality for the Bradley family. St. John's is a small city. While it is the provincial capital and houses the largest population in the province, it still possesses the familiar quality of a large fishing station/seaport town. It's not impossible, but it is very difficult to be anonymous and get lost in a crowd at St. John's. Even at major events like the St. John's Regatta, people move through the gathered throngs and meet friends, neighbours, acquaintances, and family members. Similarly, the downtown strip of nightclubs and bars is so tightly knit, it's hard to go downtown without bumping into familiar people.

During the accelerated events of 1994 and 1995, the Bradley family were still living in St. John's. The newspaper and other media coverage, while slaking the public's thirst for information, was upsetting for the family. Wounds could never completely heal, old scars and memories were reopened and brought back, forcing people to relive the devastation of December 1981, and the false hope of January 1986.

Eighteen

IN 1999, THE RCMP Major Crimes Unit, assisted by the Rovers' Ground Search and Rescue Team from St. John's, returned to Maddox Cove Road and swept the site where Dana's body had been found. Reportedly, the investigators were again looking for the alleged murder weapon.

RCMP Constable Christine MacNaughton told reporter Dannette Dooley, "We received a tip from a person who remembered seeing something years ago that he thought we should look at. The searchers combed the bushes and the trees around the site," however, "the area has really grown in over the years." The passing of time was conspiring in favour of the killer.

"Upon being assigned this case, I quickly became aware that this was a massive undertaking," MacNaughton says today, "with hundreds of existing documents to be read, to fully comprehend the previous investigative work completed by innumerable police officers over the years. Having knowledge of the investigation as a whole allows one to assess what leads and avenues of investigation to pursue, and then in what priority."

Constable MacNaughton revealed she had been helped in the investigation by the RCMP's Violent Crime Analysis Branch in Ottawa, now called the Behavioural Sciences Unit. A criminal profiler had come to St. John's and accompanied MacNaughton to the site where Dana's body was discovered. "He and I went for a drive," MacNaughton said. "We started at the point where she was picked up on Topsail Road. I drove a route through the city. We ended in Maddox Cove – what they call the pit – where Dana's body was found."

MacNaughton parked her police cruiser in roughly the same location where the suspect vehicle was spotted, and the two RCMP officers walked to the location where Dana's lifeless body had been found.

"It felt surreal as we stood there in silence. You couldn't hear a sound. I was trying to imagine what had taken place eighteen years earlier, what happened here. It's rare that I get captured in such a moment, but I felt it that day," Cst. MacNaughton said.

As part of the in-depth analysis, the profiler considered everything from autopsy reports, photographs, weather conditions, and suspect and witness statements. The RCMP were also now utilizing the so-called "ProfilerPlusDNA" testing strategy. The evidence from the Bradley case had been sent to various labs throughout Canada for re-examination. In addition, a computer analysis specialist was assisting the local RCMP in its efforts.

Breakthroughs in DNA evidence testing meant whatever limited physical evidence there was from the Bradley case, was continuously being retested. Mitochondria DNA might allow the very old unknown hairs recovered during the investigation into Dana's slaying to be re-examined with this new technique.

The RCMP were considering sending exhibits from the Bradley crime scene to a lab outside Canada for testing. Jack Lavers had made sure these hairs recovered during the Bradley murder investigation were safely kept for such a possibility.

"Of course all the hair samples were saved and still saved to this day. In order for our lab at the time (1981) to do more than the similarity check in terms of texture and similarity, they would have had to destroy the exhibit hair to make any more definitive match than they were able to do. And, I would never approve of that kind of testing that would in any way put at risk the hairs that we had, because we knew DNA was coming, even though we had some very good suspects where we knew we had to make the decision.

"Whether or not we were going to, in the process of making the match destroy the exhibit or not, the decision was always no, we would wait. And we'll see someday whether that was a good idea or not," Lavers concluded.

Whether the unidentified hair samples will ever help solve the crime remains to be seen. Time will tell. But what if the murderer dies before the police can register a conviction?

One suspect the RCMP were keeping tabs on in relation to the Dana Bradley murder had died in Vancouver, British Columbia. Constable Christine MacNaughton revealed the person of interest had died a year earlier in the greater

Vancouver area, but the officer didn't release the person's name to the media.

MacNaughton also stated the RCMP still had "a handful of prime suspects." Unfortunately, it seemed all the new technology in the world was not helping the Mounties get any closer to apprehending the killer. But MacNaughton stressed the Bradley case was still a high priority and was "not on the back burner." Tips were still coming in from the public on a regular basis.

An entire room at RCMP headquarters in St. John's is used to hold exhibits, artifacts, photographs, evidence and files from the Bradley case. Constable MacNaughton works out of the Bradley Room every day.

This room contains the school books Dana was using a few days before she disappeared, as well as maps of St. John's with possible routes the driver may have taken. A photograph of Dana stares down from the wall, silently imploring the RCMP to hunt down the evil fiend who stole her young life and future. Another of the exhibits in the Bradley Room is an exercise book with *Le Francais* written on it. This was Dana's scribbler for notes taken in French class. However, the first page of the notebook contains no French homework, but a note to her best friend Penny.

In school all the girls wrote notes in their scribblers. This way it looked like the students were sharing school material and not actually passing notes. After Dana's body was found and the murder investigation started, the police came in and collected notebooks and scribblers from students for possible evidence and leads.

It was upsetting to go through this procedure, which seemed invasive. "This all happened, and yet we were expected to go on as if everything was normal," a friend of Dana's said. "We didn't have anyone to talk to, or any grief counselling or anything. The police also came in asking what Dana had for lunch on the day she went missing. They needed to know for the autopsy." The forensic examiner would have tried to determine the time of death by discerning the contents of Dana's stomach and what had been digested.

The police were well-intentioned in trying to search for any clues as to what might have happened to Dana, and the administration and teaching staff of I.J. Samson did their best in trying to help the students cope with this intrusion. The staff talked to the students about the need for this action. The very serious nature of what had happened to Dana, and the police investigation left many students emotionally upset.

Despite the large collection of artifacts and evidence in the Dana Bradley room, as the 1990s ended and a new century began, the murder was still on the books as unsolved.

Nineteen

IN APRIL 2000, Constable Christine MacNaughton took hairs of unknown origin from the Dana Bradley investigation to LabCore Mitochondria DNA Laboratory in Raleigh, North Carolina. She brought along the 10 hairs, in hopes of obtaining a DNA profile. Mitochondria DNA testing was unavailable in Canada.

Constable MacNaughton carried samples of Dana's DNA with her, as well as known DNA from several suspects in the case. The RCMP officer was optimistic. "It is hoped that Mitochondria DNA testing will be able to reveal a DNA profile suitable enough to allow us to compare suspects to these ten unknown hairs," she said.

Apparently, Mitochondria DNA profiling was first used in a court of law in Canada in November 1999 when Newfoundlander Shannon Murrin was put on trial in

British Columbia for the death of Mindy Tran. Murrin was later acquitted and is currently writing a book about his experience.

Mitochondria DNA analysis is based on samples taken from muscle, bone, hair, skin, teeth, or fluids such as blood. While ordinary DNA analysis is found in the nucleus of a cell, Mitochondria DNA examinations focus on the material around the cell nucleus. A profile could be gained from a hair without a live root.

This advanced technology was welcomed by the RCMP, particularly Constable Christine MacNaughton. These unknown hairs are just a portion of the primary physical evidence in this homicide.

"These 10 hairs in question do not possess a root ... so we have not been able to obtain a DNA profile from the actual hairs to be able to compare them to suspects. But here we are, 19 years later, and the technology now exists, called Mitochondria DNA," MacNaughton said.

If DNA could link a question hair to a suspect, MacNaughton and her co-workers might just be able to make a stunning breakthrough in this decades-old case. Unfortunately, this cutting-edge DNA analysis alone would not be able to guarantee a conviction. The Mitochondria DNA, however, would be another tool available to investigators in their ongoing hunt for Dana's killer or killers.

Whatever the outcome of the DNA testing, MacNaughton told the media the Bradley file will continue to be actively pursued. Clearly, the RCMP continued to be relentless and tireless in their efforts to track down the evildoer who murdered Dana.

"If the technology of DNA changes," MacNaughton said, "then you have to keep entering new DNA methods into evidence. You have to continually bring it into Canadian courts. We do not hesitate on its credibility. We are very comfortable with it here and are very confident in all the laboratories ... and what this type of DNA can do for us."

The hairs, if stored in preservative solution, can last for decades without breaking down. Jack Lavers's decision to save the hairs of unknown origin from damaging testing in the 1980s seems to have proven to be a good move. Obviously, there was so little physical evidence recovered during the investigation into Dana's murder that these hairs are crucial pieces of information.

Both the FBI and the RNC have completed offender profiles in relation to the Dana Bradley case. The results of these profiles match. More importantly, perhaps, the offender profiles match suspects in the case. Unfortunately, over two decades have elapsed since Dana went missing and was found dead, and technological advances have been unable to provide the level of detail needed to apprehend and convict the guilty party.

PUBLICLY, NOT A LOT seemed to happen with the Bradley case in the year 2001, aside from a newspaper story in early December recalling the events of Dana's disappearance and murder.

The following year, the unsolved murder of Dana Bradley made front-page news when it was announced that the Dana Bradley story was to be told on national television. The announcement was accompanied by a photo of Constable Christine MacNaughton with CTV's Tom Clark, of the investigative program W5.

The journalist was in St. John's with a film crew, conducting interviews for the special. The notion of doing a documentary on the decades-old murder came from CTV Producer Brett Mitchell. He had apparently heard about the case from an RCMP contact, and the program aired on December 6, 2002 and was titled, "The Ghost of Dana Bradley."

Clark interviewed many sources, including Jeff Levitz, Jack Lavers, Constable Christine MacNaughton, Harry Smeaton, and David Somerton. Dana's friend Terri initially agreed to an interview, but changed her mind.

While the story focused on the unsolved murder, not even superficial insight was provided into who Dana was, of her talents and strengths. Dawn Bradley did not speak on camera, nor did any of Dana's school friends or even a teacher. It is reasonable to conclude that those closest to Dana found the thought of speaking about her tragic death on national television a daunting task.

Harry Smeaton thought the *W5* program was a "good effort to get it out there." The show might trigger someone's conscience. Smeaton says he has continued to talk to various media over the years, never worrying for his own safety despite warnings from friends.

"Someone jokingly said, 'You were on TV. The killer will come after you.' I said, 'Why would anyone come after me? I stated I'm not sure about the killer; I couldn't put my finger on him in a court of law.'"

During the program, David Somerton was asked bluntly by Tom Clark if he had killed Dana Bradley. Somerton's response was, "I most certainly did not." When asked if he knew who had killed the young girl, Somerton replied, "No I do not, and if I did, the RCMP would know within two seconds."

The program revealed information about David Somerton's 1986 confession to the RCMP. Jack Lavers said, "Well, there are certain descriptive things that Somerton talked about in his interview that caused me to wonder how he was able to describe those things ... His description of how he said he did this, was consistent with certain things that we knew."

For his part, David Somerton told W5 he confessed to the murder "to get them (the RCMP) off my back and let me out of that room (the interrogation room)." Mr. Somerton told W5 he had grown anxious and desperate after having been held in the RCMP interrogation room for so long. "After being there for eighteen hours, and I knew that I was flipping, on the verge of flipping out myself, because I was in a suicidal state in that room ... I said that either you do it now, have me charged or get me the 'F' out of this room before I do damage. And then I started telling them where the car was. And then I told them where the murder weapon was." *W5* made it clear the RCMP had not eliminated Mr. Somerton as a suspect in the murder case.

When interviewed months after the program was aired, Constable Christine MacNaughton repeated that position. "David Somerton, as of today, has not ever been fully eliminated as a person of interest in this file."

Around the time David Somerton confessed to the murder, Harry Smeaton looked at a lineup of police photos. "There was no one in the lineup that I could testify in court 'That's him.' But there was one photo in the lineup that I was stuck on. It was Somerton. But my brother John had a different outlook on it."

After more than two decades, the question remains. Who killed Dana Bradley?

Twenty

BETWEEN THE LATE 1970S and early 1980s, at least five other women had been murdered and/or gone missing on the island of Newfoundland.

Dana's case was not unique. "Dana was not the only one," newspaperman Bill Callahan points out. "Other women also went missing. There were Newman and Louvelle in Corner Brook and three more in St. John's. I have never been satisfied there wasn't a link between them. It seemed there was a pattern. And, it seemed to me that the justice system did not want to go there. This was hanging out there like a cloud and no one wanted to go there."

Callahan went on to make a valid point concerning the murder of Dana Bradley in relation to these other cases, which all happened from 1978-1984, a six-year period.

"People say that this sort of thing does not happen in Newfoundland, it's foreign. But there were six women killed or went missing in a space of time. Two in Corner Brook, and four in St. John's. I have never seen a succession of similar such incidents," the veteran journalist said.

Callahan's point is well made. One cannot dismissively think somehow Dana Bradley was the only young women to go missing from the streets of St. John's. Sharon Drover went missing in late December 1978, Janet Louvelle on February 6, 1979.

Both the Sharon Drover and Janet Louvelle cases pre-dated the Dana Bradley murder. Yet, as Bill Callahan correctly points out, when Dana went missing and was found murdered, many people made the comment this sort of thing doesn't happen in this province. Newfoundlanders' false sense of security had been shattered twice in the three previous years.

The tragedies continued close in succession. In 1982, Henrietta Mille, a 25-year-old native woman from Labrador, lived in St. John's. She went missing on or about December 10 and was never seen again. Twenty-year-old Marilyn Ann Newman of Corner Brook was brutally murdered on January 14, 1983. One year later, Pamela Ann Asprey, age 20, disappeared on or about November 12 from downtown St. John's. She has not been seen since.

Bill Callahan wonders why there hasn't been a more public display of rage about this string of missing and murdered women. "It's the kind of thing where women are just disappearing off the streets and nothing seems to be done. There's no public outcry, no overt evidence of extreme police measures taken when these four young women disappeared from the streets. I can't believe it."

As Managing Editor of *The Evening Telegram,* Bill Callahan wrote a regular column called "The Way We Are." In one such column, Callahan tackled the issue of the fates of these women.

> "The RNC has files on three other young women who simply disappeared off the streets of St. John's in a six-year period – Sharon Drover ... Henrietta Mille ... and Pamela Ann Asprey. But without a crime scene, without a body, without weapons, not even the space-age techniques of the RCMP Crime Lab are likely to tell us what happened to them."

Callahan's point was well made. In an interview in August, 2003 issue of *MacLean's* magazine, criminal profiler Kim Rossmo stated that geographic profiling of criminals, his speciality, is an "information management strategy, not X marks the spot." Rossmo went on to tell the magazine that "it doesn't solve a crime. You need an eyewitness, a confession or physical evidence. A profile can't do that ... it's only an information management technique."

THE CLOSENESS OF THE DROVER, Asprey, and Mille's disappearance dates to Dana's murder led authorities to consider if a serial killer might be on the loose.

Inspector Jack Lavers made sure all were re-examined. "Asprey, Mille and Drover were all Royal Newfoundland Constabulary cases, but all were reinvestigated thoroughly with the Bradley case."

AT THE BEGINNING of the twenty-first century, Robert Durnford and Malcolm Cuff were serving time for the 1983 murder of Marilyn Ann Newman. One of them, Malcolm Norman Cuff was now arraigned and convicted for the earlier, 1979, murder of Janet Louvelle. In the long list of possible suspects in the Bradley murder, Cuff was eliminated because he had been working in Corner Brook the day Dana went missing.

In January 2000, *The Newfoundland Herald* ran an investigative story on the status of the three missing women. It stated the RNC were treating the three cases as possible homicides, but with no evidence there was little they could do. However, this article stated neither the RCMP nor the RNC ruled out the possibility the cases were linked.

While there might be some element of closure for the families of Marilyn Ann Newman and Janet Louvelle, the families of Dana Bradley, Sharon Drover, Henrietta Mille and Pamela Asprey have nothing but questions. While they can try to get on with their lives, they will forever be scarred by the horrible events that had befallen their loved ones.

For the Bradley family, closure by way of a criminal conviction has not yet been provided. They can take some small hope from the Janet Louvelle murder case, though, which was actually older than Dana's murder, and was finally solved.

For the Asprey, Drover, and Mille families, there are only questions. What happened to these three other women?

Sharon Drover

When 17-year-old Sharon Drover went missing in 1978, more than six weeks had passed before her disappearance was reported to authorities.

Sergeant John House is with the Criminal Investigation Division of the Royal Newfoundland Constabulary. He first examined the missing-women cases in 1990.

"It's not inconceivable that they're linked, but we have no direct evidence to suggest that they aren't, either," House told the media.

Sharon Drover went missing in the first week of December, 1978, but incredibly, she was not reported as such until February 13, 1979. The missing-persons report came from Sharon's social worker, who had received an inquiry from Sharon's foster mother in Conception Bay South.

In December, 1978 Sharon had been living with her boyfriend on Livingstone Street in St. John's. This man was questioned by police and told them he thought Sharon had moved back home with her foster mother. Thus, he hadn't thought she was missing. Similar to the Dana Bradley case, the long delay in the start of the investigation was a setback for the police.

Initial media reports of the Drover case related the girl was on her way to her place of work at McDonald's restaurant on Kenmount Road and never made it there.

Two brothers came forward in the early 1990s, their memories jogged by media publicity. These men indicated they dropped a girl off on Long's Hill near Livingstone Street at approximately 2:00 A.M. The witnesses indicated they remembered seeing the girl walk toward her house, but then she encountered a group of young men on the street. Sharon spoke with at least one of these people, then ran to the end of Livingstone Street and down Long's Hill.

Sergeant John House told *The Herald*, "Because of personal circumstances in the lives of these two men, they had reason to remember the period of time and the year. Although I'm not certain this was Sharon Drover, it certainly appears quite likely it was her." House told *The Herald* having the two witnesses come forward shifted the focus of the investigation, because the police now think Sharon made it home that night. That is, if indeed that was the night she went missing. Like the Bradley case, there are a great many unknowns with this case.

The Royal Newfoundland Constabulary attempted to eliminate some of the unknowns in 1993 when Sergeant House contacted an RCMP officer in British Columbia, an expert in ground-penetrating radar. This officer went to the house on Livingstone Street where Sharon Drover lived in 1978, but this search proved unproductive. Following that, the police decided to remove the floor of the house and search under it.

"There were certain avenues of investigation that arose that led us to believe that it would be prudent to conduct a more thorough investigation of the premises," House told *The Herald*.

However, the search yielded nothing.

Sergeant House has checked with the Department of Social Services in every province and territory, and of course has also checked with police forces across the country. Sadly, there is no trace of Sharon Drover to be found.

HENRIETTA MILLE

Like young Sharon Drover, Henrietta Mille wasn't reported missing for several weeks. It is thought she went missing on or about December 10, 1982. Ms. Mille, 25 years old, was of Inuit descent and originally hailed from Nain, Labrador.

She went missing from the Key Club in St. John's. On the last night witnesses saw her at this club, Mille was sitting at a table with three men. At some point, Mille had told another person at the club she was afraid of these men.

Later, the club manager saw a purse on the floor under some tables. It was Mille's. The purse contained her keys, her bankbook, and other personal information. She never returned to the club to ask about her purse, and Sergeant House thinks it is a clue as to when the young woman went missing. No witnesses could be found to say when Mille left the club, if she left alone, or with the men. The police again hypnotized witnesses to see if they could recall any further helpful details, but they could not. What happened to Henrietta Mille is still a mystery.

PAMELA ASPREY

Pamela Asprey, age 20, was reported missing by her roommate on November 14, 1984. She had gone missing two days prior.

Asprey was last seen getting into a large, dark car in front of the National War Memorial in downtown St. John's. She hasn't been seen since. The driver was described as being of a large build. He was wearing a ball cap at the time. The police arranged for the witness to be hypnotized, hoping to get a more detailed description of the car. No positive outcome resulted.

Police have searched across Canada with other Police Departments, Social Services Departments, and Motor Vehicle Registration centres. Nothing.

The Royal Newfoundland Constabulary had even produced an information sheet in foreign languages which was circulated to sailors in places like Portugal. Since Asprey went missing from the downtown area, so near to the waterfront, it was thought a foreign sailor might have known something about the girl's disappearance.

To this day, authorities have been unable to find out what happened to Pamela Asprey. "We were never able to pin anything down," Sergeant John House told *The Herald*. "If, in fact, she was picked up and met with foul play, we haven't yet pinned down who may be responsible."

Similar to the Bradley case, the lack of physical evidence hampered the investigator's efforts to discover the truth about the whereabouts of Pamela Asprey. In Dana Bradley's case, the police at least had Dana's body and some eyewitness accounts. But it was as if Pamela Asprey had just vanished.

Sergeant House told *The Herald* he thinks somebody knows something about Asprey and what happened to her. For now, Asprey's file, and those of Henrietta Mille and Sharon Drover, are in the hands of the Royal Newfoundland Constabulary's Major Crimes Section.

SERIAL KILLERS

One of the foremost authorities on serial killers is Dr. Elliott Leyton of the Anthropology Department of Memorial University of Newfoundland. Leyton, who teaches a course called "War and Aggression," has been consulted by many police forces over the years. His book, *Hunting Humans*, examines multiple murderers, both serial killers and mass murderers. By definition, serial killers kill several victims over a period of time, while mass murderers slay many victims in the same violent outburst.

While serial killers and mass murderers may grab headlines, they actually only account for about two per cent of all murders.

Hunting Humans, Leyton says, examines the murderer who seeks neither profit nor bureaucratic advancement. This is the killer who kills for killing's sake, "... which nets the killer a substantial social profit of revenge, celebrity, identity and sexual relief."

Leyton argues throughout his book the motives behind the serial killer are to be found deep within the social order. He writes:

> "Our multiple murderers transcend mere catharsis and temporary gratification; their aim is a more ambitious one, a kind of sustained sub-political campaign directed toward 'the timelessness of oppression and the order of power.' But their protest is not on behalf of others, only themselves; their anguish is trivial, not profound; and they punish the innocent, not the guilty."

Quoting the psychiatrist Lunde, Leyton observes the most significant difference between mass murderers and the killer of a single person "is a difference in their relationships to the victims, the former killing strangers, the latter killing intimates."

While Elliott Leyton would not comment specifically on the possibility of a serial killer being responsible for Dana's murder and the missing women, he did make some general comments about murders, what factor or factors contribute to a murder going unsolved by police, or what factors make it difficult for police to solve a murder.

Leyton states, "The degree of relationship between killer and victim is usually the key factor. When someone kills a stranger, someone with whom he has no traceable connection, the chances of solving a murder become much reduced."

In his 1992 work *Violence and Public Anxiety,* Leyton and his co-authors write that from 1953-1984, more than 85 percent of homicides in Newfoundland occurred in the context of a prior relationship between the offender and the victim. That is, in most cases, the victim had some type of relationship with their killer.

When Jack Lavers was asked to identify the single biggest problem or hurdle the police faced in trying to solve the Bradley case, he responded, "Well, it was a combination of factors."

One of the factors Lavers proceeded to outline was the apparent lack of relationship between Dana and her killer. "... there was no connection, never any real connection or bridge that we could make between Dana and the killer. In other words, it wasn't an acquaintance, it wasn't a family member, it appeared to be some disconnect."

Assuming the perpetrator in Dana Bradley's murder had indeed been preparing to bury the young girl's body before being scared off, if he had successfully completed this gruesome task, Dana would be a missing person like Drover, Mille and Asprey. But it may well be that whoever killed Dana Bradley had nothing to do with the disappearance of the other women. Like the Bradley case itself, there are many unknowns in the deaths and disappearances of these women, many unanswered questions and many unresolved outcomes. Of course, the RCMP and the RNC may have a much better idea of things than they have released to the public.

Dr. Leyton makes the point that multiple murders are rarely drawn from the ranks of the truly socially oppressed. Most serial killers are white men who are employed and "sometimes have reasonable expectations of 'brilliant' futures."

Leyton further writes that the "killers were drawn from the ranks of the upper-working and lower-middle classes: they were security guards, computer operators, postal clerks, and construction workers." At the same time, the typical victim of a multiple murderer in contemporary times was "more likely to be drawn from middle-class neighbourhoods: university students, aspiring models, and pedestrians in middle-class shopping malls."

It can be seen that some of the details around the Bradley murder fits Leyton's description of a typical victim of a multiple murderer: a pretty young girl from a good family, who disappeared from the affluent, growing neighbourhood of Cowan Avenue. However, the three missing persons cases do not fit Leyton's depiction of the typical victim. These women vanished from the downtown area.

Leyton goes on, "multiple murderers are not 'insane' and they are very much products of their time ... the arrival of the multiple murderer is dictated by specific stresses and alterations in the human community ... he is thus a creature and a creation of his age." He also writes the "multiple murderer ... appears at special points in social evolution, during periods of particular tension." That is, Leyton argues multiple murderers are the by-products of the society and time period in which they live.

In terms of the multiple murderers he studied in the mid-1980s, specific social characteristics are found in their backgrounds. The killers Leyton studied experienced huge pressures and strains within their family of origin. All possessed one of four social characteristics: "adopted, illegitimate, institutionalized in childhood or adolescence, or with mothers who were married three or more times." Leyton insists children need to grow up feeling they have some place in the social order in order to behave normally. A disruptive upbringing impacts on a young man. Coupled with a burning yet stunted ambition, the stage is set.

> "... the future killer experiences a kind of internal social crisis when he realize he cannot live his version of the American dream. When the killers reach that existential divide, the seed is planted for a vengeance spree.
>
> On the surface, it appears they do it for the thrill of sexual excitement or the intoxication of conquest. The truth is they do it to relieve a burning grudge engendered by their failed ambition ... Others wish to live and tell their stories and bask in their fame: they usually come to be called serial killers."

Leyton paints a grim picture of an ambitious young man with high hopes for a bright future that are somehow stunted by social forces beyond his control. Seeing others to blame for his failure, the multiple murderer decides someone has to pay.

Was Dana Bradley and the other three missing women murdered by a serial killer? Was this killer getting ready to bury Dana, and got scared off, leaving her to be found? Was the killer apprehended for another crime, and unknowingly the police stopped the disappearances? Or, do the authorities have some idea what happened to Dana and the three missing women? Is the killer basking in his success at having so far eluded capture and outwitted the police?

There is room for theorizing a serial killer was operating in the late 1970s and early 1980s in Newfoundland. It is no wonder the RCMP and the RNC "have not ruled out the possibility of the Bradley homicide being linked to one or more of the three missing women cases being investigated by the Royal Newfoundland Constabulary." (Danette Dooley, Dec. 11, 1999, *The Newfoundland Herald.*)

Conclusion

HOW DOES ONE WRITE a conclusion or summary to a book about the murder of Dana Bradley? The story is *incomplete*. Crucial questions remain unanswered. Who killed Dana Bradley? Was it indeed a stranger, as the "best evidence" hints? Or, was it someone who knew her, as is the case with most homicides in Canada?

How is it this person has been able to elude the RCMP and the RNC, both of whom were assisted by magnificent public support and thousands of tips? Is the killer still alive?

What was the motive behind Dana's murder? Was it premeditated, or was it a spontaneous event in the midst of an attack on a young girl who has been described as "feisty and without self-esteem problems"? Dana was confident, outgoing and assertive. Her grade nine teacher believes she would have tried to defend herself from an attack she saw coming.

Did the killer, if indeed there was only one individual involved, intend to bury Dana? Was this man spotted along the Maddox Cove Road late on the night of December 14, 1981?

Was Dana's murder related to any of the other three missing-persons cases that are still on the books? Two other women were murdered in Corner Brook, one of them two years before Dana, another two years later. Were these slayings related to Dana's murder and the Drover, Mille, and Asprey cases? Was a serial killer stalking the confined hunting grounds of insular Newfoundland?

All these and more questions remain. Dana's family has no closure. Her friends and schoolmates remain haunted. The public remembers, and still demands a solution to the heinous crime.

To summarize and conclude, I feel it best to leave with poignant comments from key individuals interviewed in the course of research for this book.

JACK LAVERS

Jack Lavers retired from the RCMP in 1986, and is enjoying his new career as a lawyer. In 1981, he was the RCMP inspector responsible for serious crime in the St. John's area subdivision. Up to that time there were two to three murders per year, but they were usually solved relatively quickly. However, he said, it was not unusual for a young person to be murdered.

Indeed, we know that in Corner Brook, on Newfoundland's west coast, the young Janet Louvelle went missing in February 1979. Her body was found about four months later by a wildlife officer on patrol along a woods road near Corner Brook. Malcolm Norman Cuff was charged with her murder in December 2000. Cuff was already serving a life sentence for the 1983 slaying of 20-year-old Marilyn Ann Newman of Corner Brook.

The Louvelle case began like the Bradley case, as a missing-persons. Then, with the discovery of her body, it became a murder investigation. Jack Lavers actually reviewed the Louvelle case around the time it happened.

"I can remember reviewing the Louvelle case ... it was older than the Bradley case. It gives hope the Bradley case may one day be solved. But it's not only that one ... there are other cases across Canada quite old getting solved from time to time."

New advances in DNA may someday make the difference in cracking this case. "We knew DNA was coming. We had some sense of what DNA was going to do, but we certainly didn't have it at that point (1981)," he says.

There was no one single challenge to solving the crime. "It was a combination of factors," Lavers thinks. "The fact we were about a week late starting from the time she disappeared. We generally assume that, and I think rightly, that she was killed on the day she disappeared. There was no hard evidence that she was kept in captivity or kept alive for any particular period of time. So if she was murdered that day ... then we were four or five days late in getting started."

Another thorn in the investigators' side was the fact that there was another person who "was picking up young girls on the side of Topsail Road area at that time," Lavers said. As the Bradley investigation started, some young girls came forward and identified what turned out to be the wrong man. "It took us about three to four days to apprehend that person. We found out that person was not the real one we were looking for, so there was some delay and confusion in terms of composite drawings and things of that nature that was confusing from the beginning."

Further hindering the investigation was the fact they could not make a connection between Dana and her killer. As Dr. Elliott Leyton says, "when someone kills a stranger, someone with whom he has no traceable connection, the chances of solving a murder become much reduced."

The weather also posed a problem. The winter of 1981-1982 witnessed vicious storms and raging winds. Snowdrifts could have obscured a car hidden along an old woods path. Ice on a pond might have shielded a car that had been driven into it.

Apart from the weather, the suspect vehicle provided its own set of peculiar problems for investigators. "We determined we had a partial license number and a good description of the vehicle. They were all in agreement as to the type, year, model and make of the vehicle, with a little difference in terms of how people saw the colour," Jack Lavers said.

However, motor vehicle records proved problematic because of inconsistencies in recording the make and model, and because of changing over from one file arrangement to another. As investigators wrestled with car records, time was slipping away, and the perpetrator had time to destroy evidence or move away.

"DNA would have been very helpful," Lavers said. By today's standards, this technology was far behind, and the

RCMP were faced with trying to solve a murder using very little physical evidence.

The killer had time to cover his tracks. "This was the thing. We didn't have a car, we didn't have a weapon. We didn't have fingerprints. We didn't have anything. The only physical thing we had was some hair, and you know that could be suspect hairs or it could not be suspect hairs, but that's all we had. We knew she was picked up by a person in a vehicle, and beyond that you didn't know much for certain."

Another problem plaguing investigators was the eyewitness accounts. The Smeaton brothers and the eyewitnesses on Maddox Cove Road were not able to identify the suspect. Both sets of witnesses had momentary, fleeting glimpses of the car and driver, made at a distance in low-light conditions.

"The Smeatons weren't able to ID him," Jack Lavers says. "That's understandable, after two, three years. Pretty darn hard to go back and ID somebody you saw four or five years earlier, just casually.

"The people who saw him on the side of the road in Maddox Cove didn't know there had been a murder. They didn't know for another week. They thought he was out chasing a moose or something. To fast-forward that another three to four years and put them in a lineup and say this is the fellow ... it's tough. You can't really expect that. If they said, 'Yeah, that's definitely him,' then you'd be saying to yourself, 'How sure can they be?' Unless there's some outstanding physical mark that they could rely on."

After all these years, this case still affects Jack Lavers personally. "It did, and it still does affect me personally" he says. "I think about it from time to time, and I'm still very interested in it and I still help the RCMP whenever I can. The murders and capital crimes you solve, they're kind of put away. But this particular case ... because of her age, the circumstances, the fact it was a very brutal murder that remained unsolved over a long period of time, with such substantial effort on the part of everybody, and the interest of not just the people working on it, but the community, it has to remain part of your life ... because you gave such a large part of your life to it."

CONSTABLE CHRISTINE MACNAUGHTON

Christine MacNaughton has been working on the Dana Bradley murder case for the past seven years. I asked her why there is so much public interest in this case.

"This was the murder of an innocent 14-year-old girl in Newfoundland, just prior to Christmastime," she said. "Hitchhiking was not uncommon at that time, and this community was shocked as people realized that this could have happened to one of their children. It shattered local people's notions of the safety of where they lived. This was a presumed abduction and murder of an innocent teenager, and it made many families feel vulnerable. We here in Newfoundland don't want to think this type of crime could happen."

What factor or factors make it hard for police to solve a murder like the Dana Bradley case? "A witness's memory can fade as years go on, or key witnesses may pass away," MacNaughton said.

"Over the most recent years of my career with the RCMP, I have worked on in excess of a dozen homicide investigations. Working on the Dana Bradley investigation has made me realize what it means for a family to lose a child and that no matter how many years pass, the family cannot ever put closure to such a horrific event in their lives. All the police officers who have worked on this homicide over the years have been very passionate in their pursuit of bringing this investigation to a successful conclusion one day, not only for justice, but for the family of Dana Bradley."

Constable MacNaughton says the family is kept informed of the unfolding investigation. "Investigators keep an open line of communication between the police and family, while attentively being sensitive to their needs."

Asked if the family and friends of Dana Bradley should take hope from the recently solved Janet Louvelle murder case, Constable MacNaughton says, "In any lengthy murder investigation involving a loved one, there will always be hope. The family of Dana Bradley can take solace in the fact that this will never be closed until this is one day solved."

The Bradley case is worked on continuously. As new tips pour in weekly, they are investigated agressively and thoroughly on a daily basis. MacNaughton was firm. "Investigators will continually strive to bring this investigation to a successful conclusion one day, not only for justice, but for Dana's family."

Glenda Cluett

In the case of Dana Bradley's grade nine homeroom teacher, "Dana comes to mind every school year. Over the years since it happened, someone always calls looking for an interview. It haunts you."

Cluett recalls an unnerving experience she'd had a year or two after Dana was murdered. "I went to see Shelley Stokes, a psychic in St. Phillips. I had a reading done, sitting at her table. I never knew the woman. When I was leaving, I happened to pick up an ornament she had on display. She told me, 'That belonged to Dana Bradley.' It was very eerie. Shelley was spot-on about the things she told me. She picked things out."

In the days and weeks following Dana's murder, Glenda Cluett dreaded seeing Dawn Bradley, Dana's mother. "I used to worry about upsetting her."

PAT DOYLE

Pat Doyle was the reporter on duty for *The Evening Telegram* on Friday, December 18, 1981, the day Dana's body was found. It did go through his mind after a few weeks that they might never solve it. "They seemed to have the body and nothing else," Doyle said.

HARRY SMEATON

Today, Harry Smeaton reflects on everything that happened. "I mulled it over in my mind. What if we had got the (full) license plate? Maybe it might not have prevented the tragedy, but maybe it would've brought closure and helped apprehend whoever did it.

"He (the murderer) was a coward to do what he had done. I thought it over, over the years, that maybe we could have prevented it. It's one of the what-ifs. It was a more innocent time in Newfoundland."

Mr. Smeaton is still affected by the murder of Dana Bradley. "It's a crazy thing. Every year or six months I get calls about it;

someone wants to do an interview ... But I don't mind talking with the media, because it might help in some small way."

Harry Smeaton firmly believes some person has knowledge of the crime and has just not come forward. "I think someone out there knows something. It goes through my mind very much."

BILL CALLAHAN

Bill Callahan, who as a journalist took a proactive role in bringing the case to the public, is still upset when the subject of the unsolved murder comes up.

"It brings back distressing memories. Some of my children knew her. She lived on Patrick Street, but hung out in this general vicinity," he said.

Bill Callahan says it might be gleaned from the news the thing was not tackled as it should have been "At the paper, we didn't feel enough effort, or resources, was put into it.

"I think I felt it would have been solved post-haste. She was seen in town getting in a car and the driver was seen. It doesn't seem rational that in a small town like this the murder was not solved."

FRED TULK

Dana's school principal is still haunted by the event. "Everything came to nothing. No one got closure. Even if today I meet students, they say, 'Sir do you remember ...'

"The not knowing the why, the who ... that really freaked us out. I thought at first they'd get the killer. But as time went on I realized there was no closure. The police put everything they had into it. But there was a lack of closure."

Following Dana's murder, Mr. Tulk saw more parents picking their children up after school. "There was a newer understanding of safety; it became the key concern. Afterwards there was an emphasis put on (the dangers of hitchhiking) by staff."

DANA'S FRIEND TERRI

"Myself and Dana grew up together with another friend. Then we met Penny in junior high school," Terri says.

Terri never thought Dana's murder would go unsolved for so long. "I still find it quite astonishing for a small city like this one that there are no credible leads for them to go on. Every Christmas I used to get a call from the police, discussing some new lead, asking me to look at pictures and mug shots. It's amazing for such a small city. It's unbelievable."

When I approached Terri for an interview, I was apprehensive about bringing up sad memories. I asked Terri what she thought of me writing this book.

"I think it's a good thing. I wish there was more publicity on the case. If no one does anything on it, the case will just go cold. *W5* and the book may be positive (influences on the case) and are an excellent idea," she said.

DR. ELLIOTT LEYTON

The noted criminologist was tight-lipped when it came to commenting on this specific project. Obviously, Leyton is sensitive to the fact that the Dana Bradley case, as well as the three missing-persons cases, remain unsolved. As such, public comments could jeopardize the outcome of events. However, he did offer some insight into homicides in general.

"It varies, but in general something like 75 to 80 per cent are solved. (This is) much higher in Newfoundland, I would think, where most killings are between those who are well known to each other."

"The typical murder in Canada," Leyton says, "is either a spouse-killing (usually a wife) or a friend/associate (usually male). Each of those constitute around a third of murders in Canada. Most murders occur in the home or in an area with bars and clubs. Shooting is only one-third of murders in Canada, although it is the largest single category. The remaining two-thirds use knives, fists, cars, drownings, poison, et cetera."

Who is the typical murderer in Canada? Elliott Leyton answers this question in his 1995 book *Men of Blood*. "They (murderers) are ... young, single, male Caucasians. The majority (87 percent) of suspects are male, 40 percent are under 25, 45 percent are single, and 76 percent are Caucasian."

Clearly, the Dana Bradley homicide case does not fall into the category of a "typical" murder.

What motivates someone to kill a 14-year-old schoolgirl. Dr. Leyton: "Sex and power thrills, probably. And utter inhumanity."

In his 1986 book *Hunting Humans*, Leyton comments on the issue of a murderer's inhumanity.

> "The fundamental act of humanity is to refuse to kill. Our murderers have consciously rejected that humanity ... For their betrayal of humanity they deserve no better fate than to be permanently excised from the social order. Their only value is as objects of study."

Writing *Hunting Humans* was a deeply disturbing experience for Elliott Leyton: "Not just because I was forced to witness such terrible suffering, but also because I was able to glimpse just how powerless police can be in their attempts to find these new murderers in the anonymity of the modern world."

This was a tough book to write. The subject matter is depressing. A young girl murdered: no killer apprehended. Two police forces unable to catch the killer.

How does the story end? Will the murder of Dana Bradley ever be solved?

There's an old saying in St. John's that the Southside Hills can predict the weather. When the Hills look close and foreboding, a snowfall can be expected.

It's a pity the Southside Hills can't talk. What a story they could tell.

The Ghost of Dana Bradley

The Dana Bradley tragedy is one that lingers on in the minds of Newfoundlanders. Nearly twenty years after her death, Ron Hynes, one of the province's most respected songwriters was startled out of sleep one night and was amazed at the images, sounds, and words that came to mind. He went downstairs and spontaneously began writing. A song that had been internalized, written subconsciously, was set free and put to paper, begun and finished in ten minutes.

The song came about because "she was so young, her murder was so brutal, and it got into the collective consciousness and stayed there," Ron says.

It was such a personal song and Ron felt somewhat uncomfortable about it. He was content to leave the song unpublished, unperformed, unless it met the approval of Dana's mother. In one of his most difficult performances, he sang it privately for Dawn, who upon hearing it, encouraged him to sing it in public.

The Ghost of Dana Bradley

The Ghost of Dana Bradley
Is standing sadly on the road to home,
You can see her as you hurry by,
Pale against the evening sky;
She stands alone,
Thumb out to hitch a ride,
Swallowing her young girl's pride like a bitter wine,
Counting on a kind heart.
There's a gamble at the start in these times.

I read her name in the *Daily News*,
Heard it on the radio,
It was on TV;
Someone stole her life away,
Someone still at large they say,
Who can he be?
How does he sleep at all,
Face to the guilty wall, remembering?
Does her sweet face haunt his dreams,
Or does he even feel a single thing?

Is there not a Christ on high?
Is that just another lie we've fallen for?
And is justice not a dull-edged knife?
Is there but hard life and nothing more?
Hard life and nothing more.

The Ghost of Dana Bradley
Is waiting patiently for someone,
You can see her as you hurry by,
Pale against the evening sky;
She waits alone,
Thumb out to hitch a ride,
Swallowing her young girl's pride like a bitter wine,
Counting on a kind heart.
There's a gamble at the start in these times.

Is there not a Christ on high?
Is that just another lie we've fallen for?
And is justice not a dull edged knife?
Is there but hard life and nothing more?
Hard life and nothing more.

The Ghost of Dana Bradley
Is standing sadly on the road to home,
You can see her as you hurry by,
Pale against the evening sky;
She stands alone,
Thumb out to hitch a ride,
Swallowing her young girl's pride like a bitter wine,
Counting on a kind heart.
There's a gamble at the start in these times.

Depending on the kindest heart,
Could be a gamble at the start in these times.

Recorded on the CD Get Back Change: Borealis: 2003

Darrin McGrath is a free-lance writer. He has a Master's degree (Sociology) from Memorial University of Newfoundland, where he taught for a number of years. He has written for a variety of newspapers and magazines including: *The Telegram*, *The Northern Pen*, *The Monitor*, *The Downhomer*, *The Navigator*, *Outdoor Canada* and *Explore*.

Hitching a Ride is his third book. His other titles include *From Red Ochre to Black Gold*, and *Last Dance: The Knights of Columbus Fire, December 12, 1942*.

Darrin lives in St. John's with his wife Ann and their three dogs.